J's
Everyday
Fashion &
FAITH

J's Everyday Fashion & FAITH

PERSONAL STYLE WITH PURPOSE

Jeanette Johnson

Waterfall
PRESS

Published by Waterfall Press, Grand Haven, MI
www.brilliancepublishing.com

Amazon, the Amazon logo, and Waterfall Press are trademarks of Amazon.com, Inc., or its affiliates.

ISBN-13: 9781503942943
ISBN-10: 1503942945

Cover design by Faceout Studio
Cover photography by Joshua Johnson (www.joshuacjohnson.com)

Printed in the United States of America

Contents

Introduction

"Why do I do these things to myself?!"

An email reminder that I was scheduled to speak at a church had just come through. It wasn't on my calendar, and I had totally forgotten that it was only a few days away. And I was seriously wondering why I had agreed to do it in the first place!

Don't get me wrong. I genuinely enjoy public speaking and giving style seminars to groups. I've traveled across the country to give them, and I enjoy making people laugh and providing helpful tips about shopping and putting outfits together. But I must've been out of my mind when I said yes to doing a style seminar at a local church.

Because Jesus and style are like oil and water: they just don't mix. Or at least that's what I grew up believing. As I was raised in a conservative Christian home, somewhere along the way the message of my heart became "Fashion is bad." I don't recall anyone actually saying that out loud, but all signs pointed in that direction. Growing up, spending money on clothes was not encouraged, because fashion was considered superfluous. Bible verses commanded women not to care about their appearance for the sake of vanity. And ultimately a life of faith focused on helping others who are in need, not spending time and money on self-seeking things like our own clothes.

Certainly, fashion *can* be bad. An unhealthy focus on personal style can do everything from hurt the environment—by creating unnecessary waste—to foster a conceited sense of self and entice us to obsess over vanity, and it can destroy our financial well-being by overspending. Peruse fashion magazines or social media and you'll see how fashion is portrayed: Luxury is king. Celebrities are our idols. Every new trend is coveted, and at breakneck speed. And yet here I was, marching into a Baptist church to give style tips to a group of Christian women. I'm sure I was challenging myself to face my fears when I agreed to do it, but now that the day was here, I just wanted to run in the other direction.

To help work through those nerves, I sat down the night before the style seminar and typed up a quick blog post about my journey of balancing my faith with a career in fashion. The personal nature of the post deviated pretty far from my usual "outfit of the day" type of blog posts, so I wasn't sure how it would be received, but the response knocked my socks off! Women were emailing me and telling me their stories in person—it turns out that I was not alone and that so many women were on a similar path. They were passionate about personal style, hair and makeup, creativity, and the arts, but they also felt some discomfort and shame in pursuing these areas personally or professionally because of their religion or personal values. And then, not two days later—an email arrived from a publisher: Would I write a book on this topic?

I immediately thought: *Absolutely not.* I barely survived the style seminar! But like a toppling line of dominos, saying yes to that style seminar at a church set into motion what would become the book you are reading today. I gave the style seminar, and I didn't die. And when I sat down to brainstorm ideas for a potential book, I realized just how many pressing topics there are to consider about the subject of fashion and faith. And so I threw my hat in the ring: *Put me in, Coach!*

In so many ways, I am the unlikely author of this book. Which is also a line you'll find in the "About Me" section on my blog, because I feel like the unlikely author of pretty much anything pertaining to fashion. I grew up in Kansas and lived on a dirt road surrounded by farms. No one in my family was into fashion. (Unless you count the threadbare sneakers full of holes that my dad wore as "fashion.") I wasn't even that into fashion myself, at least not in practice. I loved magazines but hardly ever experimented with personal style until college. For a brief time, I enjoyed fashion immensely and even showed promise of being good at it. (I was awarded "best dressed" in my sorority, which was probably just a nice way of saying, "You're trying harder than everyone else.")

And yet for as much as I enjoyed clothes in college, I struggled with them too. I found myself stuck between two worlds. Within the context of my faith and my values about money and beauty, I felt guilty buying clothes, even if I really needed them. In my early twenties, I tried earnestly to sit out the topic of fashion altogether, to disastrous effect. I had a string of embarrassing faux pas, including running into my ex-boyfriend and his new girlfriend while wearing a Teletubbies T-shirt (it was a free T-shirt, guys, and I was on a budget!). I also lost a promising job opportunity because I was too cheap to buy a proper suit. I had numerous embarrassing situations at work when I realized I was dressed like a teenager, so no one was taking me seriously. And while living in Boston, I failed to properly dress for the elements, which meant I was often miserably cold.

As I entered adulthood and started my career, a new message about fashion was emerging—that clothing can't be avoided. In our critical, appearance-driven society, clothing is an important form of nonverbal communication that can mean the difference between landing the job or not, even if that's completely unfair. (And it can prevent the allover body numbness that accompanies walking to work in freezing-cold Boston winters!)

But style goes so much deeper than just keeping us warm and helping us find success at work. I'm talking about the fundamental questions of a woman's heart and her longing to feel beautiful. How do our self-esteem and self-worth fit into the picture of personal style? And what if you're like me, and fashion is your art form, a precious part of your soul

3

where you long to be creative and express yourself through beauty? Can this passion play out in a healthy way within the context of our faith?

The turning point for me—that is, the compromise that allowed me to honor both my faith and my art—was setting a clothing budget, which we'll talk about in detail in chapter 8. I finally felt free to explore the creativity and passion that had been there all along. I went deeper and deeper into the fashion world, unlocking a joy I hadn't experienced before, and eventually started my fashion blog, J's Everyday Fashion, in 2010.

While my mission for my blog has always been about providing a place of positivity and light in the fashion-journalism industry, this is my first time broaching the subject of fashion and faith. Because even with a clothing budget and a clearer understanding of how to balance the two, I still cowered anytime I met someone in a Christian setting like church. I either wouldn't mention what I did for a living, or I'd immediately launch into a little spiel about why it's possible to love Jesus and blog about fashion.

I'm sure my obvious insecurities convinced no one, because I still needed to settle the relationship between these two personal fundamentals myself. I needed to find a balance and a reckoning between the faith I was raised in and my love for Jesus, and the career and hobby that I love and believe I was made to do.

I set out to write this book not to convince readers of what's in my heart or that I'm doing "fashion and faith" well. (I realize that it could be easy to come away with the complete opposite impression.) Instead, writing this book was an important part of my own journey. In order to reconcile the tension between fashion and faith in my life, I needed to ask the tough questions and study Scripture, and in doing so I found a peace I had never thought possible. I hope by sharing that journey with you here, along with stories from other women, I can help people like me find a little peace and resolution in their own journey too.

I'm also excited to share the new twists and turns my fashion journey has taken lately. For more than six years, the mission statement behind my blog has been "fashion on a budget" and "the look for less." When you read about my personal journey with money, this will totally make sense: growing up in a super-frugal household, I felt excluded from fashion because of my socioeconomic status, and J's Everyday Fashion has always been about bridging that gap and making an online magazine where everyone feels included. By re-creating celebrity outfits for a lot less and rebelliously doing side-by-side comparisons of my outfits next to theirs, I set out to prove that you don't need a million bucks to achieve the same look.

Recently, several relationships and experiences were placed in my path, which I believe were a total God thing. I found myself traveling to Haiti and India, where I learned more about the garment industry, immersing myself in the topics of fair wages and clothing's impact on the environment. I came away with a fresh outlook and a sense of global responsibility that I'm excited to share with you in chapter 9.

Whether you're a hairdresser, an artist, a stylist, a dancer, or a writer—and whether the arts are your vocation or your hobby—I hope that this book resonates with you. I hope that by sharing some of the struggles I've had reconciling my faith and my art, I can in turn help you with yours. I want to balance the desire for fun personal style with respect for my faith and values, and I'm guessing that you do too. And I do believe that we can have both! Let's be balanced and enjoy a creative life while maintaining a sense of diplomacy and charity. Let's once and for all determine what is a good, gentle nudging from our conscience, and what is raw, unabashed guilt, which is foe and not friend.

I hope to build a relationship with you, even if we never meet face-to-face, and I hope that you will consider sharing your stories with me too.[1]

---

[1]   I would love to hear from you at j@jseverydayfashion.com or on my blog, www.jseverydayfashion.com.

So, how can we justify our passion for fashion, or any creative venture, in a broken and hurting world? Let's dive right in and find out.

Chapter 1

Does God Approve of Fashion?

My pastor's wife has the prettiest pink earrings. Sitting two rows behind her in church the other day, I was admiring the bubble-gum color and chandelier shape. They made a big statement against her porcelain complexion, blonde hair, and small frame. She and her family are renovating their house right now, and she convinced her husband and their three sons to paint the front door hot pink. Because, why not?! I love her style. She has great taste, and she embraces her creativity fully.

Not two seconds after I admired those earrings did that little familiar voice creep in, though. *Fashion guilt.* I wondered: *Was it okay for her to wear such loud, colorful earrings in church? Should she be spending time and money on something so frivolous?* If I sound judgmental, I'm not, at least toward other people. In spite of that nagging voice in my head, I think my pastor's wife has every right to wear those earrings and would even go so far as to argue that they are an expression of worship, of showing up for church in a way that's meaningful to her. But even though I can easily defend her fashion choices, I can still be pretty hard on myself.

In this book, I will make the case that clothing is a necessity, that (like it or not) it's essential to our role in an appearance-based society, and that it's an important part of our relationship with our own beauty.

I'll also advocate that fashion can be an inherent part of our precious soul, that it can be done with the utmost financial responsibility, and that it can even be used to solve world problems.

But before we dive into those topics, let's address first and foremost our most important question: What does God say? How does our Creator feel about the subjects of art, creativity, and fashion? Above anything else, does He approve of fashion?

God, the Original Artist

We often refer to God as "Creator," but have you ever stopped to reflect on what that word really implies? In Genesis 1, God spends seven days creating the heavens and the earth. He creates lightness and darkness, day and night, the sky, water, dry ground, the sun, the moon, and the stars. On day five, God really starts showing off. He dedicates an entire day to creating the animals that roam the earth:

> And God said, "Let the water teem with living creatures, and let birds fly above the earth across the vault of the sky." So God created the great creatures of the sea and every living thing with which the water teems and that moves about in it, according to their kinds, and every winged bird according to its kind. And God saw that it was good. (Genesis 1:20–21, NIV)

Maybe we've heard this story so many times that it all sounds kind of like no big deal. Like any person doing their job, God showed up to work and got the whole "creation thing" done in seven days. But the creation story speaks to something much deeper than that. God, it seems, is the original artist.

Sometimes it's hard for me to imagine that the creation story is less about austerity and more about total, mind-blowing creativity, but then I consider the beauty of the Grand Canyon, with its peaks and ridges and reddish colors that melt into achingly beautiful sunsets. Or the coral reefs teeming with electrifying, neon fish darting about sponges and corals. Or the way that spotting an elephant in the wild causes our heart to skip a beat, not because we are fearful but because something within us compels us to drop everything in reverence.

God wasn't just doing His job. He could've given us a mundane landscape, with no mountains, no lush scenery, no coral reefs, and animals for purely practical reasons. But have you ever seen a wombat or a platypus—they are hilarious! Or consider the majestic way horses' muscles ripple in the sunlight as they run. Or think of the terrifying, strange creatures that live in the darkest depths of the ocean. Or the animal babies that melt our hearts in YouTube videos and internet memes. When I recall the way plants and flowers cover every inch of the earth in beauty, creating spectacular natural landscaping, I think about a God who is so clearly an artist. As our Creator, He was not just "getting the job done." As the original artist, He is creative, passionate, thoughtful, clever, meticulous, and a total visionary.

You may be wondering why. With all the problems in the world, doesn't God have better things to do? Why would He expend so much time and energy just being creative and making things "pretty"? There are so many reasons, but the first is that God delights in beauty Himself.

Before there was an audience, before man and woman even existed, God took time to appreciate beauty. At the end of each of the seven days of the creation story in Genesis, He takes a moment to enjoy and evaluate His art. The phrase "and God saw that it was good" is repeated six times in Genesis 1, in verses 10, 12, 18, 20, 25, and finally in verse 31, when God reflects on all seven days at once: "God saw all that he had made, and it was very good" (NIV). Like any earthly artist, God not

only enjoyed the process, but He enjoyed the end result and took time
to reflect and appreciate all the beauty that He had created.

He had more than His own delight in mind, though. In so many
ways, His creation is a gift to us: thoughtful provisions in preparation
for the man and woman He knew would soon be joining Him on his
newly created earth. As any artist might put extra care into making
a guest room aesthetically pleasing for their anticipated houseguests,
God had the delight of our hearts in mind as well. In the same way
that God delights in beauty Himself, He also approves of and urges
our own delight in it.

Genesis 2:9 makes it clear that the trees are not only for food, but
for aesthetics, as well. "The Lord God made all kinds of trees grow out
of the ground—trees that were pleasing to the eye and good for food"
(NIV).

The idea that God intends for us to relish in the beauty of His
creation purely for our own delight can also be found in John Calvin's
writings from the 1500s. Calvin says that food, clothing, and vegetation
are there for not just necessity, but also for our enjoyment—simply so
that we can delight in the beauty of their appearance, and that they can
bring us "good cheer."

> Now if we ponder to what end God created food, we
> find that He meant not only to provide for necessity
> but also for delight and good cheer. Thus the purpose
> of clothing, apart from necessity, was comeliness and
> decency. In grasses, trees and fruits, apart from their
> various uses there is beauty of appearance and pleas-
> antness of odor.

How does Calvin know that? He says the answer is right in front
of us and can be found in the natural qualities of the things themselves.
Why would flowers be so beautiful to look at, and food so delicious to

our palate, and clothing so uplifting to our spirits, if we were not meant to enjoy them in some way?

> Scripture would not have reminded us repeatedly, in commending His kindness, that He gave all such things to men. And the natural qualities themselves of things demonstrate sufficiently to what end and extent we may enjoy them. Has the Lord clothed the flowers with the great beauty that greets our eyes, the sweetness of smell that is wafted upon our nostrils, and yet will it be unlawful for our eyes to be affected by the beauty, or our sense of smell by the sweetness of that odor? Did He not so distinguish colors as to make some more lovely than others? Did He not endow gold and silver, ivory and marble, with a loveliness that renders them more precious than other metals or stones? Did He not, in short, render many things attractive to us, apart from their necessary use?[1]

Beyond our personal enjoyment and enjoying beauty for the sake of beauty, God also uses his artistry and creativity as an important reminder of Him. God often seems very far away, and communicating with Him can be frustrating or feel impossible. One way God chose to bridge that gap is through His creation: the delights of the earth so we can see Him and be reminded of Him. Like little love notes strewn about, creation is a gentle reminder that He's there, that He loves us every day. He woos us with these love notes, like a whisper in the breeze during a sunset, or in the heart-stopping moment when a wild animal comes into view.

---

1   John Calvin, *Institutes of the Christian Religion*, ed. John T. McNeill (Westminster: John Knox Press, 2011), 721.

One of my favorite books is the autobiography of Joni Eareckson Tada. At the age of seventeen she was involved in a diving accident that left her paralyzed from the neck down. Her incredible memoir is about overcoming obstacles and turning our darkest times into light. But one anecdote from her book really stuck with me.

Joni was on vacation with her family in Canada. As a result of her accident she was confined to a wheelchair, so, one sunny morning when her family went out for a hike, they set her up with a book to read. Her arms were paralyzed but with a little maneuvering she could turn the pages of a book with her chin. As luck would have it, Joni knocked the book over mere minutes after her family left. She sat there in angst for hours, not able to move or do anything other than reflect on the scenery around her. She prayed for something—anything to occupy her mind—a buzzing bee or a graceful butterfly. But nothing ever came.

That night as the family sat around a campfire, a curious bear suddenly entered the scene. Joni was not afraid, and the bear got spooked and left shortly thereafter. But in that exciting encounter Joni felt that God was answering her earlier prayer, and that it was a dramatic reminder that even in her altered state, He was still with her. Maybe she couldn't go out and seek wildlife herself, but if the girl wasn't going to the bear, then God was going to bring the bear to the girl. I'll never forget her delight in recounting the story.

I can relate to Joni's excitement when I witness an animal in the wild in all its glory. One evening during our honeymoon cruise in Alaska, we were dining in a fancy restaurant. During the appetizer course we spotted orca whales out the window and totally forgetting my highbrow surroundings for a moment, I jumped out of my seat, pressed my nose against the window, and squealed like a child. I have even stronger feelings toward bears, although I don't like them nearly as much as Joni does. On the same trip, we were out hiking in Juneau and our path collided with a black bear. I was so terrified that my mind went completely blank and I ran. It was a magnificent brush with nature; at least, it felt that way once I was confident we had survived.

I will be happy if I never see another bear that close, but in the day-to-day I am always seeking out wildlife encounters. We even bought our first home on a property where we could regularly spot animals. In our Florida backyard, we love catching glimpses of alligators, otters, owls, bald eagles, turtles, snakes, and fish. And my husband and I tend to opt for vacations that involve animals and natural beauty—whether it's sailing in Hawaii, snorkeling in Roatán, or hiking in Alaska.

And why is that? Because I simply can't wait to catch a glimpse of Him. Those little reminders of our Creator's passionate creativity speak to my soul in a way that is tough to put into words. He is just so awesome in that way—I admire Him for so many reasons, but to me His artistry is one of the surest and truest connections to my heart.

We only need to look so far as the mountains, flowers, and animals here on earth, and the elaborate imagery of heaven written in the Bible, to see God. In Psalm 19:1, it says: "The heavens declare the glory of God; the skies proclaim the work of His hands" (NIV).

And we delight in these things because His own beauty shines through them. In Psalm 29:2, it says: "Give unto the Lord the glory due to His name; worship the Lord in the beauty of holiness" (NKJV).

And these things remind us of His infinite power and love for us. In Psalm 8:3–4, it says: "When I consider your heavens, the work of your fingers, the moon and the stars, which you have set in place, what is mankind that you are mindful of them, human beings that you care for them?" (NIV).

One of my favorite comments I've ever received on my blog sums it up so perfectly:

> I think sometimes society, and maybe even the Christian community today, discounts beauty and art as not being important, or at least not near as

important as other things . . . But it's obvious through animals, the sky and nature that God is ALL ABOUT beauty for its own sake. He loves it!—LG

God's passionate creation of our universe was not without good reason. He not only delights in the beauty of His creation Himself, but He also made it to delight us: simply for the delight itself and to bring us "good cheer," but also as a powerful way of communicating His love and His heart with us here on earth. The earth, the sky, the animals, and the ocean are all a compelling and important reminder of Him for us to enjoy.

Art as the Antidote

When I was five years old, I underwent a second surgery to remove cystic hygromas, which are viciously malignant tumors. Within a couple weeks of developing, the tumors had wrapped themselves around my esophagus so tightly that I couldn't eat solid food. The surgery, like the tumors, was dangerous, the doctor telling us I had a 50 percent chance of survival each time. I was only three during the first surgery, so I don't remember much, but every detail of that second procedure is etched in my memory forever: waking up to see my Garfield suitcase and balloons at the foot of my bed, the sterile smell of the hospital, the taste of the food my grandpa would sneak in from my favorite restaurants, the colorful toys in the kids' room that I was too weak to play with, and the painful tube that stuck out of my neck for weeks.

During that second surgery, my doctor paused to ask my parents for permission to continue the surgery at a later date. He could see more tumors, but they were too deep, and I had been under anesthesia too long. They closed me up quickly, and everyone expected that I would have a third surgery soon. But that third surgery never happened.

While I was still recovering from the second surgery, my parents took me to a prayer revival. I remember lots of sweaty hands and people speaking in tongues as they prayed for my healing. And on the next doctor's appointment, CAT scans showed that the tumors were gone. The masses that my doctor had seen had disappeared, with no medical explanation.

We often see people on the news that have a unique zest for life because they survived a bad accident or beat cancer. That zest came at a very young age for me. In some of my earliest memories, I was very tuned in to my own mortality and how fragile life can be. My body had been through battle, and I had a central role in what my family felt was a supernatural miracle and an incredible answer to prayer. Oftentimes this experience causes me to relish the little things, the proverbial stopping to smell the roses and delighting in the beauty of God's creation. My experience as a child manifests today in my love for the outdoors and wildlife, and in my fascination with color, both in nature and in art. I embrace the beauty and the lighthearted things in this world because I'd been in such a dark place at such a young age.

And yet my experience as a child also resulted in a strong sense that the world has very real problems. I don't take the subjects of fashion and beauty lightly, because I know what else is out there: sickness, disease, war, poverty, starvation. I carry these things around like a heavy backpack, and they often weigh on my conscience so much that I don't feel right about indulging in the lighthearted.

Which is where the tension really lies, the two sides that create friction. Do we embrace beauty because life is short and every day is a wonderful, delicious gift? Or do we drop frivolous pursuits and instead take up our swords to battle the problems in this broken and hurting world?

The short answer is that we should surely embrace both. Ecclesiastes 3:1–8 tells us that "to every thing there is a season, and a time to every purpose under the heaven."

[There is] a time to be born and a time to die . . . a
time to break down and a time to build up, a time to
weep and a time to laugh, a time to mourn and a time
to dance . . . a time to embrace and a time to refrain
from embracing . . . a time to keep silence and a time
to speak . . . a time to love and a time to hate, a time
of war and a time of peace. (KJV)

At first glance, it may seem that we should keep our seasons separate, bottled up in their own jars, to be used independently of one
another. But is this verse actually encouraging us to embrace both
simultaneously? During times of war, should we also not embrace
moments of peace? During times of mourning or sadness, should we
also not embrace moments that make us laugh or inspire us to dance?
We may hear of cancer survivors who say, "Singing got me through
this," or of someone who lost a child taking painting lessons to help her
cope. Embracing *both* the serious and the lighthearted can be beneficial,
or even necessary, in the darkest and most challenging times.

When the deadliest mass shooting in modern American history
happened here in Orlando in 2016[2], artists responded by doing what
they do best: creating beautiful things. Colorful murals were painted in
remembrance throughout the city, bringing beauty to spaces that once
were bare. Dancers and singers dedicated performances to the victims
of the shooting and rallied people together to heal.

But, you may ask, when there are bombings and shootings and
war, how could God possibly have time for frivolous pursuits like art,
fashion, and beauty? Shouldn't He be out preventing crimes? When

---

2   Peralta, Eyder, "Putting 'Deadliest Mass Shooting in U.S. History' into
     Some Historical Context," *The Two-Way*, NPR, June 13, 2016, http://
     www.npr.org/sections/thetwo-way/2016/06/13/481884291/putting
     -deadliest-mass-shooting-in-u-s-history-into-some-historical-context.

we ponder this, we are often overlooking the important role that our freedom and ability to make choices has here on earth. Because of our freedom, God won't physically stop a person from committing a crime, in the same way that He wouldn't force you to commit a crime. God is all-powerful and omnipotent, He has the final say and ultimate control over this world, but He has also granted us freedom, and He honors that even to the point of not always being able to save us from danger.

Our having freedom and choices removes God as the puppet master of our lives and places Him as the hero of our story, as the general of our daily battles. He would love nothing more than to heal all children from disease and to stop violent crimes, but the forces of evil cannot always be stopped due to the spiritual battle that is being waged all around us. Victory over evil was won with the resurrection of Jesus, but the surrender has not yet fully been realized. It is much like how we may declare victory over a world war here on earth, and yet evil still marches on, and war crimes are still committed. Victories from the spiritual war must be enforced and are the crucial part of the story we are living in right now.

That's why our actions—our prayers, our faith, even our art—matter so much, because we are fighting right alongside God and his heavenly host of angels, and our actions have an impact on this daily struggle with the darker forces of the world. When we pray, when we worship, when we create art, when we dance, we give our positive energy and sustenance to a spiritual battle being waged around us. Think of the movie *Elf* when Jovie encourages the people of New York to sing Christmas carols—those carols and the people's belief that Santa Claus is real actually gives Santa the fuel he needs to fly his sleigh. 1 Thessalonians 5:17 commands us to "pray without ceasing" (ESV), and for good reason. Our prayers and the art we create contribute in a positive way and help combat evil, both tangibly and in the spiritual world. One day everyone will be clothed in righteousness and everything broken will be restored to beauty; but even now, living in the period before that, there can be amazing acts of beauty among destruction. When evil leaves its mark, we often rush to bring beauty to the scene, with an inherent understanding of the virtue it bears.

In 2015, terrorist attacks rocked Paris to its core[3]. Much like what we saw here in Orlando, in the days following the attacks in France touching stories of hope emerged. Passersby filled bullet holes left in windows with beautiful roses, and placed lit candles and left decorated cards for the bereaved. In one particularly moving story, a man sat down outside of the Bataclan music hall at a grand piano and played "Imagine" by John Lennon[4]. In a place surrounded by destruction, the pain and magnitude of the ugly crimes committed there seemed to hang in the air like a gray cloud. But as he played, beautiful sounds filled the air, and the music seemed to take on an entity of its own, breathing life into the neighborhood.

I can picture God beaming with joy at that scene. During times of mourning, playing a piano may not be the first thing that comes to mind, but beauty doesn't necessarily take away from the "important things" like battling evil; in fact, it only helps us enforce the victory of the larger spiritual war. Our creative expression can be a sort of a medicine for evil, or an important antidote. Playing a piano helped Parisians rise from the ashes, collect themselves, and move forward.

The music, the roses, the art—they give us hope and a renewed spirit, and encourage us to keep pressing forward. Robin Williams's character in the movie *Dead Poets Society* says: "Medicine, law, business, engineering—these are noble pursuits, and necessary to sustain life. But poetry, beauty, romance, love—these are what we stay alive for."

---

3   Jeremy Diamond, "France and Nigeria: 2 Countries Rocked By Terror with Very Different Reactions," CNN, January 13, 2015, http://www .cnn.com/2015/01/13/politics/paris-nigeria-attacks-comparison.

4   "Pianist Plays John Lennon's 'Imagine' outside Bataclan Concert Hall— video," *Guardian*, November 14, 2015, https://www.theguardian.com /world/video/2015/nov/14/pianist-plays-john-lennon-imagine-outside -bataclan-paris-attacks-video.

When it comes specifically to fashion, it can work in a similar way. As women, we are in a never-ending struggle to see ourselves as beautiful. With such deep concerns at hand like self-esteem and self-worth, it is no wonder that the Enemy has often capitalized on it, attempting to make the topics of beauty and fashion sinful and unholy.

Women are exploited for beauty and taken advantage of for their beauty. Fashion as an art has the power to affect the battle that plays out around us and in our hearts and minds, between good (seeing your own beauty) and evil (the dark voice that denies the true source of our beauty, or tells us that it doesn't exist at all). When women undergo transformations of their outward appearance, the power that is unleashed by those aesthetic changes often brings light to their hearts and those around them, changing them from the inside out. (See more in chapters 4 and 5.) Our decision to wear a beautiful silk fabric or a brightly colored shirt can be our way to express worship to our Creator, to show our support for a cause, and to defy the negative voice that tries to keep us from seeing the beauty that God has created in us.

God has so many things to care about, for sure. But in His omnipresence and His omniscience, God also sees beauty as a worthy pursuit. When we shut out the idea of beauty completely, we fall victim to a trick that evil plays to keep us in the darkness; we resist embracing the light that counteracts the evil. God not only made beauty for His own pleasure, for our pleasure, and to serve as a reminder of Him, but also as a method of winning the biggest battle of all: the daily struggle between good and evil.

When God Loves Us Through Fashion

In my early twenties, I wanted a pair of True Religion jeans so badly. As much as I wanted them, I couldn't bring myself to buy a pair. With exorbitant Boston rent to pay on my first-job-out-of-college salary, spending three hundred dollars on jeans did not feel like being a good steward of money. So when I found a look-for-less pair at a local boutique for around thirty dollars, I was beyond ecstatic. As I stood in line to pay for them, I did a happy dance and prayed, "God, thank you so much for this blessing. You knew how much I wanted those jeans, and you provided a way for me to have them on my budget. Thank you, Lord!"

And then it came. The voice that said, "You've got to be kidding me. God has way better things to do with His time than to help you find a stupid pair of jeans." I felt so incredibly foolish. I immediately thought of all the hurting people in the world, who really need God's help. How could I have been so selfish to think that finding the perfect pair of jeans had anything to do with God? Not only was I ashamed that I thought God would care, but really, I wondered if He would even want me to be buying myself jeans in the first place. The idea I developed in childhood that "Fashion is bad" came rushing back at me.

As shame poured over my heart, I looked down and read the tag sewn into the jeans. In small red print that could have been easy to miss, it said, "God Loves You." Seeing those words sucked the wind right out of me, and hot tears rolled down my cheeks.

Sometimes in moments of small faith we want God to answer us in a real, audible voice, and this was one of the few moments in my life where that actually happened. Like a denim fortune cookie, those jeans felt like my tangible proof that God and His love could somehow be tied to fashion, rather than always standing in total opposition to it.

For the most part, it is settled in my heart that God loves beauty, and He wants us to delight in it. It is settled in my heart that God loves art, and He wants us to create it. But it's harder for me to apply these concepts specifically to fashion. We may know and understand God's heart on the subjects of beauty and art, but how and when does this extend to the subject of clothes, makeup, and hair?

For me, the resistance to seeing God's approval of fashion is often rooted in two Bible passages. In what is often considered the golden rule of fashion in the Christian culture, 1 Peter 3:3–4 cautions us against outward adornment, whether that be elaborate hairstyles, gold jewelry, or fine clothes. (Ouch.)

> Your beauty should not come from outward adornment, such as elaborate hairstyles and the wearing of gold jewelry or fine clothes. Rather, it should be that of your inner self, the unfading beauty of a gentle and quiet spirit, which is of great worth in God's sight. (NIV)

In Matthew 6:25–30, we are told "do not worry about . . . what you will wear," and that if we do worry about clothes, then we have little faith in God. (Double ouch.)

> Therefore I tell you, do not worry about your life, what you will eat or drink; or about your body, what you will wear. Is not life more than food, and the body more than clothes? Can any one of you by worrying add a single hour to your life? . . . And why do you worry about clothes? See how the flowers of the field grow. They do not labor or spin. Yet I tell you that not even Solomon in all his splendor was dressed like one of these. If that is how God clothes the grass of the field, which is here today and tomorrow is thrown into the fire, will he not much more clothe you—you of little faith? (NIV)

For me these Bible passages—two of the very few that even mention fashion—seemed to slam the door completely shut on the topic.

How could God possibly approve of fashion, when I'm commanded not to worry about it at all, and when wearing stylish clothes would be engaging in the sinful act of outward adornment? Maybe I shouldn't have even gone shopping in the first place.

While Peter's command can certainly sound like a total prohibition on elaborate hairstyles, gold jewelry, or fine clothes, it's clear to me now that isn't what he's saying. Rather, he's cautioning women against using those things as the *source* of their beauty, not the act of wearing the items themselves. I no longer believe that this verse leaves "outward adornment" completely off the table. In fact, I think it leaves it open to all sorts of interpretation—enough to fill up this book. Often in life, we may have an instruction manual, but it's up to us as to how we apply it.

As for the passage in Matthew, "do not worry about . . . what you will wear" doesn't necessarily mean that dressing ourselves and participating in personal style is sinful. In fact, might it be saying that God cares so much about our clothes that He wants to take care of it for us?! That Solomon's kingly robes are no match for the "splendor" and artistry of a God who wishes to bestow His glory on us? "Will He not much more clothe you" than the flowers in the field, and dress you in "splendor"? Certainly, this passage is more about encouragement to trust God with every minute aspect of our lives, including our clothes, and is less about potential sin. So then, do we dare imagine that God actually cares so much about fashion that He would bless us with a pair of look-for-less jeans in a Boston boutique?

For me, that fateful day was about more than a silly pair of jeans. It marked a huge shift in my thinking. Could I fathom—would I dare to believe—that God could love me through fashion? And in doing so, banish any doubt I have about His approval of it? What I realized then is especially compelling, as I regularly see and hear women sharing stories similar to mine.

Take my friend from church, Ashlyn, who shared a story on her blog about the time "Jesus bought [her] a dress." Her best friend was getting married and wanted her to be a bridesmaid. It was a huge honor and one she happily accepted, but it also came with a big price tag—$260 for the bridesmaid dress. At the time, money was tight, and even the smallest unexpected expense would have put Ashlyn and her husband in the red and leave other bills unpaid. Ashlyn had just finished breaking the news to her husband over dinner when the unexpected happened.

> By the time we had finished dinner, Tim went to do the dishes and I saw I had gotten an email from my Etsy account. I literally have a couple random things listed up there, and those couple of things have sold on occasion, but it's no regular thing—at all. The message I received was from a lady who wanted to place the biggest order I'd ever received of these little balloon invitations I make. Less than 24 hours later I got another message regarding another smaller order of the same thing! It seems kind of random and a little bit silly to get excited or write a big long post about this . . . but guys, the total for the two sales came out to $266 and some change.
>
> It wasn't random. And at the end of the day, it's just money. It's not the money that is so exciting. It's the fact that, although my life and these worries are all just a mist that vanishes, and I'm just a tiny speck on this big earth that sits in an enormous galaxy, our great and glorious Father in heaven paid attention to a tiny little detail like a bridesmaid dress that I'll be wearing in a very special lady's wedding.[5]

5   Ashlyn Mattea Krall, "He's so good, right?" *Jesus Bought Me a Dress* (blog), June 24, 2015, http://ashlynkrall.wixsite.com/brickhouseonbarley /single-post/2015/06/25/Jesus-Bought-Me-a-Dress.

Several years ago I did a giveaway on my blog. A popular brand had sent me a pair of boots, and I was paying it forward by sending the boots to a reader in the form of a store credit. Little did I know what that small gesture would mean to her. Here's the email she sent me:

> I am so excited about winning this contest. It sounds silly, but this was one of those instances where God showed me that He cares even about the small things—I have really wanted a pair of boots, but it's not something that's in our budget right now, so when I got your email saying that I had won, it was an answer to a prayer that I hadn't even dared to pray.

Of course, these types of "God is in the details" stories are not always about fashion. There are so many little ways God blesses us, like in this story, from another woman I go to church with, Olivia:

> We were newly married, and even newer parents. I was staying home with Mason, and our rent was more than half of our monthly income—so that didn't leave much room for anything extra, especially not for home decor. Pinterest was new in my life, and as a stay-at-home mom, I wanted badly to make our house look like a home and really reflect us, but we had no funds to do so. Teal was a pretty big hit that year, and I had been eyeing some teal lamps, but it just wasn't an option. Michael was out on the road to pick up parts to fix our ancient dryer, and he saw this teal lamp in

the window for $1.99. He didn't even know I wanted
a teal lamp specifically, but he brought it home, and I
was in love with it. It still sits in our room, because it's
too good of a reminder to let go of.

When you think about all the worthy causes that command the
attention of the Creator of the universe in a given day, it's pretty incredible that these types of stories happen with regularity. Which is one
of the things I love most about God's heart. He may not be the Santa
Claus we sometimes imagine Him to be, or a fairy in the sky doling out
free boots, but I do believe He loves to bless us with little things from
time to time. He loves what our hearts love, the way a parent rejoices
in the small things their child delights in. It says in Psalms 37:2, "Take
delight in the Lord, and he will give you the desires of your heart"
(NIV)—whether it's a teal lamp, a bridesmaid dress, or that specific pair
of jeans. God's power is never more evident than when we consider his
attention to detail, both for beauty as a whole, and for the little things
our hearts love.

Just bask with me for a moment over this perfect description of a
God who loves details, and knows us so intimately, in Psalm 139:

You have searched me, Lord, and you know me.

You know when I sit and when I rise;
you perceive my thoughts from afar.

You discern my going out and my lying down;
you are familiar with all my ways.

Before a word is on my tongue
you, Lord, know it completely.

You hem me in behind and before,
and you lay your hand upon me . . .

For you created my inmost being;
you knit me together in my mother's womb . . .

My frame was not hidden from you
when I was made in the secret place,
when I was woven together in the depths of the earth.

Your eyes saw my unformed body;
all the days ordained for me were written in your book
before one of them came to be.

How precious to me are your thoughts, God!
How vast is the sum of them!

Were I to count them,
they would outnumber the grains of sand. (NIV)

God's opinion about fashion is not as final as I had once thought. In fact, it seems that God may approve of fashion after all. Of course, to say that He's fine with fashion as an expression of beauty and art is one thing. But how does God feel about Christians working in the fashion industry? Let's explore deeper, and answer another tough question in chapter 2, "Can Fashion Be My Calling?"

Chapter 2

___

Can Fashion Be My Calling?

For many years, Annette struggled with her vocation as a hair and makeup artist within the context of her Christian faith. As a pastor, her father was outspoken in his disapproval of her career, and an old boyfriend often shamed her, at one point writing in a letter, "Is this really the legacy you want to leave behind, of pretty hair and makeup?"

Annette is now married with two children, but you can see the pain in her eyes as she recounts those words. She absolutely wants to leave a legacy for her girls that she can be proud of, and the idea that being a hairdresser prevents her from doing so still stings. She wants to honor God with her life and her vocation, and raise her children to do the same.

Annette certainly has a worthy calling in my eyes. Hairdressers and makeup artists are, to me, magical creatures that have been blessed with skills that I simply don't possess. At the most basic level, there is no way I could cut my own hair. Unruly and thick, it puffs up like a mushroom when it's too short. When it's left too long and without layers, it's too much to manage. I spent two weeks in Africa and my hair literally developed a moldy smell because we didn't have electricity and it never fully air-dried. I couldn't function without an Annette in my life!

After years of feeling like I looked sort of "blah" whenever I did a TV appearance, I was fortunate enough to have Annette teach me how to do my own makeup. She walked me through every single step, telling me exactly what brand and color to buy, and showing me how to apply it. Thanks to her, I can now focus on the good stuff in life—the important moments like my wedding (Annette was there to take makeup and hair totally off my mind), my friends and family, and my career. Maybe to some it's just hair and makeup, but Annette lives for those moments when her clients' faces light up and she knows she's helped them see their true beauty. I can't think of why being a hairdresser with a heart like Annette's wouldn't be a worthy vocation!

Thankfully, after years of prayer and reflection, Annette now fully believes being a hairdresser is a worthy calling. I'm happy to say that her father is also onboard with her career choice, and now beams with pride as he tells members of his congregation what she does for a living. I can't help but wonder, though, would things be different if Annette's passion was for something else, like food or sports? Is a vocation in the fashion industry all that different from a vocation in another industry? And how do we choose a vocation at all—where does our desire for hair, makeup, and clothes really come from?

Not Just a Calling, But Part of Your Soul

> Red is the devil's color. If the church found out that I bought a red cape at a street fair, they would probably make me burn it. I bought it anyway.
>
> —Mary, on the TLC show *Return to Amish*

Mary sounds like my kind of girl, because I really like the color red too. And even if someone told me not to wear it, I'd be very tempted to try it anyway! Why is that exactly? Am I being sinful or rebellious, or is there a deeper desire in my heart for the color red?

My style icon, Iris Apfel, also really likes color. Now ninety-five years old, Iris spent decades traveling the globe as an interior designer for high-profile clients like the White House. Her style motto is "More is more, and less is a bore," and she really piles it on—prints, bright colors, and stacks and stacks of jewelry. There are many reasons I love Iris, but what she illustrates for me is the idea that fashion is more than a career or vocation—it can also be a special part of our personality, a precious part of our soul.

There's a scene in the documentary *Iris* where she visits a little shop in Brooklyn. It's indistinct. There are no name brands, and it looks more like a tourist stand than a department store. It's full of African prints, jewelry, and tchotchkes, and Iris is negotiating with the owner, offering something like twenty dollars for a stack of bracelets. Fashion, as we often see it in magazines, is all about labels and impressing people. The media defines fashion as what celebrities wear, what luxury brands put on the runways, and whatever trends are the flavor of the day. But Iris proves that fashion can mean something else entirely. For Iris, fashion is rendered for her own pleasure, with no thought given to the media or anyone else. Iris might be showy, but she is never "showing off" by wearing all that jewelry and color. Fashion is something much deeper than that for her. It is, quite simply, her art.

The same is true of another inspirational woman who comes to mind. Janet is a mentor to a mom's group in Windermere, a community southwest of Orlando. I heard her speak once on the subject of fashion and faith, and her experience can be summarized in one memorable phrase: "tan and navy."

Janet loves color, rhinestones, and bows—and not in small doses. When she was the organist for her church in the eighties, some of the sweaters she wore were certainly not intended for a wallflower or anyone trying to blend in! Unfortunately, some of the people in Janet's congregation were not onboard with her style. They asked her if she could tone it down, feeling that, as the organist sitting at the front of the church, she was too flashy. Perhaps they thought she was distracting from the message and the ultimate focus of church? Or they felt that her joy in her appearance was modeling vanity, a trait they didn't want one of their church leaders to possess?

Janet tried. She went out and bought tan and navy outfits, as plain as she could possibly find. She admired one of her good friends whose style was the epitome of tan and navy and pulled that look off effortlessly. If only Janet could be like her friend. But something just didn't feel right. And Janet's husband noticed.

"What are you wearing lately?" he asked. "I didn't marry tan-and-navy Janet, I married you."

I identify with Iris and Janet, because, like these women, I am also not "tan and navy." I loved my home church back in Boston more than I can say, but on several occasions I received comments about the bright colors or makeup I was wearing. What to me feels like a cheerful turquoise shirt and matching earrings that may brighten someone's day or give glory to God, others might see as vain or frivolous in some conservative or Christian circles.

Stories like Janet's and my own are, unfortunately, all too common. If you enjoy fashion and beauty from a deep part of your soul like I do, then you may often wonder, *Am I too much for Christianity?* Why do I like bright and colorful? Why can't I just be happy with tan and navy? Am I showing off? But I don't think these desires were put there on accident, and I don't think they are sinful.

I could hear the whisperings of my creative soul from a very young age. Long before I knew what society expected me to wear. Long before I understood what was "in style" or "on trend" or what the best brands were. Long before those things were in my existence, there was a desire and joy to mix colors, to play dress-up, and to marvel at the beauty of so many different fabrics at the local craft store.

When I was four or five, I asked my mom to make me a princess costume for Halloween. I remember being very specific—I wanted pink satin, as many silver and blue sequins as she could possibly fit, and a crown with a pink organza veil. I have no idea where I got those ideas, but I felt so special in that costume. I can still remember how the silky pink satin felt against my skin, and how it glistened with all those sequins. I can recall some of the first outfits I wore at such a young age—something about the fabric, clothing, and color spoke to me in a very real way.

I like to jest that I eat, drink, speak, taste, smell, and crave color. Sometimes that means picking up a paintbrush and actually making a picture on a canvas, mixing and inventing whatever colors I want using only red, blue, yellow, and white paints. More often, though, it means standing in my closet and seeing what crazy color combination I can come up with. Pencil skirts, cardigans, tops, shoes, purses, and necklaces—how many colors, patterns, and layers can I fit into one outfit? Tweed, bouclé, jacquard, leather, lace, and silk. Polka dots, stripes, paisley, chevron, and gingham. I crave these things like some might salivate at the thought of food. I'm not ashamed to say it—I take so much pleasure in mixing clothes together! It's a joy I cannot describe. If my closet ever burns down, you will not see me cry. Because these are just things, objects I've collected, tools I use to express creativity, the paints I use to paint. I don't feel an emotional connection to them at all. I do, however, feel a strong connection to the creativity and the process of putting things together.

In Revelation 21:18–21, heaven is described like this:

> The wall was made of jasper, and the city of pure gold, as pure as glass. The foundations of the city walls were decorated with every kind of precious stone. The first foundation was jasper, the second sapphire, the third agate, the fourth emerald, the fifth onyx, the sixth

ruby, the seventh chrysolite, the eighth beryl, the ninth topaz, the tenth turquoise, the eleventh jacinth, and the twelfth amethyst. The twelve gates were twelve pearls, each gate made of a single pearl. The great street of the city was of gold, as pure as transparent glass. (NIV)

Certainly we can conclude that there is a much deeper reason and a longing in our hearts for beauty, if heaven is decorated in this way.

Perhaps you identify with Iris's "more is more" philosophy and Janet's "tan and navy" story the way that I do. Or perhaps you don't. Regardless of your style philosophy, do your longings and passions have a deeper meaning for you? Can you recall memories from your childhood that may have stirred your heart in a certain direction? Or perhaps now in your adult life there are more pressing issues like a busy career or children that keep you from exploring those creative longings? Ultimately I believe those desires are valid, at their core, and are something to be celebrated. Creativity and our passions—whether that means, for you, clothes, beauty, food, or art—are an important part of our souls.

Fashion Versus Other Vocations

Art is everywhere. Maybe sometimes it gets a bad reputation as a career choice, thanks in part to the popularity of the term "starving artist," but it's really quite unavoidable. All of us are engaging in some form of art on a daily basis—whether it's singing along to the song on the radio, watching a movie, or driving a car. Design is an inherent part of our lives, and for each one of those endeavors there is an artist with a job—the musician who wrote the song, the director who made the movie, and the engineer who designed your vehicle. Artists decided the way your seat belt would fit, the slope of your ceiling, and the color of your shirt. If millions of people didn't do creative jobs, then the world would be a seriously lacking place, in so many ways.

Artistic expression and beauty, as we explored in chapter 1, are of the utmost importance to God. It's such an important topic that God included it in the Ten Commandments. In Exodus 20:4–5, the second commandment says:

> Thou shalt not make unto thee any graven image, or any likeness of any thing that is in heaven above, or that is in the earth beneath, or that is in the water under the earth: Thou shalt not bow down thyself to them, nor serve them. (KJV)

The verse uses the term "graven image," which generally brings to mind carved statues of a religious nature that people worship as "gods." But "any likeness of any thing" is referring to literally anything we create, and art of every kind. Is God telling us not to make or buy a beautiful dress, a tasty meal, or an artfully designed home? No. Rather, He is telling us not to treat them as idols and prioritize them before Him.

As I read it, any type of art is judged, according to the second commandment, in a similar way. It seems that it's not so much the subject of the art that matters to God (whether it be a graven image or a likeness of anything that is in heaven, on earth, or underwater): it's the meaning behind the artwork and whether or not we make it an idol in our lives. And yet, so often, society places fashion, makeup, and hair in a different category. An architect probably doesn't bring shame on a Christian family, but a fashion model might.

Let's imagine, for example, that a chef has a pantry with thousands of ingredients: spices they've collected from all over the world, the choicest meats, a wine cellar with an impressive catalog, and cheeses that are tough to pronounce. Are we uncomfortable with that passion? Compared to a closet full of clothes, shoes, and makeup, does that food pantry seem materialistic? Do we view the chef as greedy or having a sinful nature for collecting so many food items? If the spices were hundreds of shoes, would we judge him for having too much "stuff"?

Food is a necessity to staying alive, I'll give you that. (Clothes are also a necessity, as we'll explore in chapter 3.) But it can also be idolized and prioritized before God, the way that any hobby or artistic endeavor can. And food waste—like fashion waste—is a huge issue for our environment. Moreover, food costs time and money to prepare. You could argue that it's better to cook only for utility, using only a few ingredients, just as you could say it's better to have fewer clothes.

But let's consider two other examples, of someone who likes to scrapbook and of someone who is into sports. Should we judge the scrapbooker on how many adhesives, stencils, markers, stickers, and books they are buying and using? Or the sports fan on the amount of money he spends on team jerseys and season tickets? Do we worry about why the scrapbooker needs so many materials to create one scrapbook, or why her scrapbook is so flashy? And what's with all the face paint and team gear—why can't the sports fan celebrate his favorite team in a more subdued way?

My point is this: fashion often gets placed in a much different category than other hobbies and careers. One reason we do this is because aesthetics, rather than food or experiences, are often prioritized last and marked as being "frivolous." But God is less about practicality than we may realize.

When a woman used "an alabaster jar of very expensive perfume" to wash Jesus's feet in Matthew 26, Jesus didn't admonish her for owning expensive perfume. He didn't ask her why she wasted her time storing it in an alabaster jar (because, honestly, that sounds pretty fancy to me). His disciples questioned her about wasting the pricey perfume, saying that it should go toward something more practical, like being sold for money to go toward feeding the poor. But Jesus said, "No way, José!" (not a direct quote). He said that her alabaster jar was an act of worship so incredible that He would mark her name in the history books. (What?!)

> While Jesus was in Bethany in the home of Simon the Leper, a woman came to him with an alabaster jar of very expensive perfume, which she poured on his head as he was reclining at the table.
> When the disciples saw this, they were indignant. "Why this waste?" they asked, "This perfume could have been sold at a high price and the money given to the poor." Aware of this, Jesus said to them, "Why are you bothering this woman? She has done a beautiful thing to me. The poor you will always have with you, but you will not always have me. When she poured this perfume on my body, she did it to prepare me for burial. Truly I tell you, wherever this gospel is preached throughout the world, what she has done will also be told, in memory of her. (Matthew 26:6–13, NIV).

I am so guilty of imagining a God that admonishes any form of luxury or aesthetics. If God were to visit my house, I wonder, would He raise an eyebrow at my shiny mirrored coffee table and ask, "How much did you pay for that?" or step into my closet and say, "How many pairs of shoes do you really need, Jeanette?" And while those are totally valid questions—and everything should be in moderation, not making anything an idol, as laid out in the second commandment—God also isn't at the ready to strike down every material thing in my life like I sometimes imagine Him to be.

We explored the ways in which God appreciates art and beauty in chapter 1, but oh how quickly my heart goes from "God loves beauty" to thinking anything creative, beautiful, or artsy with fashion is simply not practical and therefore doesn't have value or much importance. And yet there was a time when churches were the most breathtakingly beautiful, ornate places on earth! It took Michelangelo four years to paint the ceiling of the Sistine Chapel[1]. That's a stark contrast to the churches that I grew up in, with little to no decoration. I'm guessing that if my church spent four years and hundreds of thousands of dollars simply to make things look "pretty" and not necessarily functional, there would be an uprising in the congregation of epic proportions. Be that as it may, I believe God reacts to an ornate church built in His honor, or pink chandelier earrings or a turquoise shirt worn as a form of worship, in the same way that Jesus reacted to the woman with the alabaster jar of perfume—with praise, not admonishment. The Old Testament is full of detailed instructions from God on how to make things not functional but instead incredibly ornate and beautiful, from the ark of the covenant to the clothing described in this passage from Exodus 28:3–5:

> Tell all the skilled workers to whom I have given wisdom in such matters that they are to make garments for Aaron, for his consecration, so he may serve me as priest. These are the garments they are to make: a breastpiece, an ephod, a robe, a woven tunic, a turban and a sash. They are to make these sacred garments for your brother Aaron and his sons, so they may serve me as priests. Have them use gold, and blue, purple and scarlet yarn, and fine linen. (NIV)

In our everyday lives, there are a couple of ways to do a self-check-in to make sure we are expressing our art in a manner that honors God

---

1   Jennie Cohen, "7 Things You May Not Know About the Sistine Chapel," History.com, November 1, 2012, http://www.history.com/news/7-things-you-may-not-know-about-the-sistine-chapel.

and His commandments. One way is by examining whether our art extends to *every single area of life*. If we're passionate about all of it—clothes, makeup, interior design, sports, concerts, scrapbooks, etc.—then we may just really like shopping.

But that's hardly ever the case—usually we are tuned into one specific type of art. I once saw a comic strip that illustrates this principle so perfectly. The main character is incredibly frugal when buying food, selecting only the cheapest household items at the store and buying only the clothes they absolutely need. But when they walk into Hobby Lobby, they turn into a totally different person, wearing a fur coat, sunglasses, and a dollar-sign pendant on a chain, and throwing huge wads of money into the air. I can relate—I'm a minimalist in almost every other area of my life. I drive the same old car, cook with only a few ingredients, hardly ever buy makeup or go to concerts, and I'm not into sports. Fashion is really the only nonessential expense in my budget. I'm incredibly frugal, so I feel okay spending a set amount of money from my budget on something that I love and feel was put into my soul from a very young age.

Another surefire way to know if something is really part of your soul, and not just a trivial pursuit that could lead us afoul of God's commandments, is to ask yourself the question that Steven Pressfield poses in his book *The War of Art: Break Through the Blocks and Win Your Inner Creative Battles*: "Of any activity you do, ask yourself: If I were the last person on earth, would I still do it?"[2]

According to Pressfield, even as the last man on earth, Arnold Schwarzenegger would be pumping iron at the gym, and Stevie Wonder would be playing the piano. His litmus test is a good way to identify the

---

2   Steven Pressfield, *The War of Art: Break Through the Blocks and Win Your Inner Creative Battles* (New York: Black Irish Entertainment, 2012), p. 158.

difference between vanity and a true passion for art, fashion, or beauty that resonates from your soul.

It's easy to dismiss fashion from the category of soulful art, especially since it's something we physically wear on our bodies. A love for clothes, hair, and makeup can be written off as something that girls do just to make themselves pretty. But ask yourself: Would you still be making outfits if you were the last person on earth? Would your soul still rejoice in the act of mixing eye shadows and lip colors, or creating new hairstyles, or whatever it is that your chosen art requires? Because if you take away "others" from your story, if they don't exist, and you still want to do it, then I would argue that it's something much deeper than simply wanting to look pretty.

As the last person on earth, I imagine I would be a lot like the character Carol from the (aptly named) TV show *Last Man on Earth*. There's no one around to impress, and yet Carol is a very flashy dresser and loves to mix prints and bedazzle things. She also enjoys drawing in her notebook and trying her hand at a myriad of DIY projects. Why does Carol care about wearing rhinestones when there's no one to see them, or take on DIY projects when there are no mom friends or Pinterest followers to impress? Why at a young age did I want to wear so many bright colors and want to express myself creatively with a pink sequined costume?

Because, for both Carol and me, even when the world has fallen silent and there's no one around to see, there's still one voice we must answer to: the calling of our souls.

The Spiritual Source of Creativity

As if my fashion *hobby* didn't make me feel guilty enough, life took an unplanned turn several years ago, and I wound up with a *career* in fashion. I didn't really mean for it to happen. I'd lost my job and couldn't find another one, so I decided to monetize my blog to pay my rent. It was never "the plan" to go into fashion professionally. I never imagined that it could turn into a career someday, let alone an incorporated business.

In some ways, I struggled more to reconcile my faith with fashion as a hobby than I do with fashion as a career. And that's because of one amazing aspect of my job: the Holy Spirit aids me in doing my work every day. Yes, you read that correctly. I know how crazy that sounds, that the Holy Spirit would bother with a fashion blog. But it's actually in keeping with a concept that is embraced widely by both secular and Christian artists.

Years ago, I stumbled upon a TED Talk given by author Elizabeth Gilbert, in which she presents the theory that creativity is not something that comes from within or is created by your own thoughts; rather, all your ideas are given to you. Gilbert calls this idea-supplier a "divine attendant spirit that came to human beings from some distant and unknowable source,"[3] but it has many names. The ancient Romans called it "genius." As a Christian, I identify it as the work of the Holy Spirit, or as a holy host of angels.

I love how Gilbert describes poet Ruth Stone's experience with creativity. It's a story that will give you goose bumps.

> When she was growing up in rural Virginia, she would be out working in the fields, and she would feel and hear a poem coming at her from over the landscape. She said it was like a thunderous train of air, because it would shake the earth under her feet. She knew that she had only one thing to do at that point, and

---

3   Elizabeth Gilbert, "Your Elusive Creative Genius," TED video, 19:09, accessed May 22, 2017, https://www.ted.com/talks/elizabeth_gilbert_on _genius/transcript?language=en.

that was to, in her words, "run like hell." And she would run like hell to the house and she would be getting chased by this poem, and the whole deal was that she had to get to a piece of paper and a pencil fast enough so that when it thundered through her, she could collect it and grab it on the page. Other times she wouldn't be fast enough, so she'd be running and running, and she wouldn't get to the house and the poem would barrel through her and she would miss it. She said it would continue on across the landscape, looking, as she put it "for another poet [to inspire]."

But even a force as thunderous and awe-inspiring as creativity has its detractors. Steven Pressfield calls creativity's great opposing force the Resistance. The Resistance is an aversion to the creative process—when everything tries to stop you from creating. Sometimes my Resistance will try to guilt me into believing that fashion is sinful, but it also runs me into the ground with practical nuisances. "I'm hungry," it suddenly says. Or, "Better finish that load of laundry." Or, "This email looks urgent . . ." And on it goes until I feel almost too tired to even start writing in the first place. But once I get past all that, and get serious, that's when the "genius," or the Holy Spirit, comes to greet me. And it's a beautiful, magical thing.

While writing this book, for example, there were moments and even entire days when I could feel an undeniable presence in the room. It takes effort to get to that special place—an open heart, time spent on your knees in prayer before you start working, distractions on lock-down—but when it greets you, it's effortless and it feels like someone is doing all of the work for you. It's not even my fingers typing any-more. It's not my hands putting together an outfit. Sometimes it's like the ideas fall out of the sky and into my eyes as things are revealed before me—colors, patterns, or the words on a page—and in awestruck wonderment toward this invisible presence, I can't possibly imagine where any of it came from.

The Bible first mentions the Holy Spirit filling someone in Exodus 31. And guess what the purpose was? For the sake of creative works, done by skilled workers! The Holy Spirit fills these workers to help them make, among many other things, "woven garments." (Mic drop.)

> Then the Lord said to Moses, "See, I have chosen Bezalel son of Uri, the son of Hur, of the tribe of Judah, and I have filled him with the Spirit of God, with wisdom, with understanding, with knowledge and with all kinds of skills—to make artistic designs for work in gold, silver and bronze, to cut and set stones, to work in wood, and to engage in all kinds of crafts. Moreover, I have appointed Oholiab son of Ahisamak, of the tribe of Dan, to help him. Also I have given ability to all the skilled workers to make everything I have commanded you: the tent of meeting, the ark of the covenant law with the atonement cover on it, and all the other furnishings of the tent— the table and its articles, the pure gold lampstand and all its accessories, the altar of incense, the altar of burnt offering and all its utensils, the basin with its stand—and also the woven garments, both the sacred garments for Aaron the priest and the garments for his sons when they serve as priests. (NIV)

The unique relationship between creativity and the Holy Spirit has not only helped me affirm my choice of work, it has also encouraged me greatly as I journey along my professional path. I'm never fearful that the ideas—the bread and butter of any creative career—will just stop coming. I've now spent more than six years blogging, and I haven't had a day without ideas yet. Knowing that my ideas are given to me by the Creator of the universe gives me peace of mind, as I'm pretty sure His inspiration won't be drying up any time soon.

Believing that God is driving your creativity also helps keep your ego in check. If I were to internalize the positive comments I receive on my blog, then the whole thing becomes about me. But instead I strive to keep at the forefront of my mind that the work isn't mine to begin with. Yes, I absolutely played a part in the process. And maybe I deserve some credit for showing up, but I'm not the creative source for any of the fashion content that I create or the books and articles that I write. I'm just the conduit.

Models for Christ

Whether or not you believe the idea that the Holy Spirit is part of any creative process, let alone a fashion creative process, is totally your call. But I am thankful for our current church home, which regularly teaches another principle—the idea that no matter where you work, your vocation can be used as an instrument in spreading God's love and word.

I'm not talking about turning your job into a platform for evangelism. In fact, evangelizing too much on the job is a good way to get yourself fired; if you were hired to fix a leaking sink, and you show up only to evangelize, there's a good chance you won't be invited back.

Instead, I'm talking about spreading God's light in other ways that are inherent to your job. Our pastor often uses the example of the trash collector that visits their house every week. He is so incredibly happy and joyful in his work, smiling and greeting people as he goes about his day, that he spreads the love of Jesus wherever he goes. He is a living example of Colossians 3:23, "Whatever you do, work at it with all your heart, as working for the Lord, not for human masters" (NIV).

Another example that is especially inspirational to me is Eric Liddell, an Olympic gold medalist and missionary whose life story is portrayed in the movie *Chariots of Fire*. He believed that wherever God puts you, you can use that as an opportunity to spread His love, and that even a calling to run track and field in the Olympics was as honorable as missionary work. In the film his character says: "I believe God made me for a purpose, but he also made me fast! And when I run I feel his pleasure."

In the fashion industry, there are plenty of opportunities to create light and positive changes through God's love. Models for Christ, a nonprofit founded in 1984, brings together fashion professionals who seek to do just that. Their website has some great testimonials from members who are successful models, makeup artists, and creatives within the fashion industry, who spread God's love and light with their vocation. One member, Virginia, says:

> Over the years working as a model, I have realized that I am a missionary in the midst of the fashion industry. I am usually undercover. Whether it be a casting, a runway show, or at a photo shoot, the Lord places girls before me who are hurting, empty and in some instances, on drugs . . . Each day I have opportunities to share Christ, watch Him set them free, receive healing in their lives, and know the love of their heavenly father.

Wendi Braswell, a personal shopper in the Tampa area, told me:

> As a Christian girl growing up I struggled with my love for fashion and wondered if it had any real value in the world. It seemed to me the church oftentimes did not reflect or celebrate a women's beauty or simply

her creative spirit. Over the years as I've grown in my relationship with Christ so has my ability to recognize that helping women develop their style is my calling! He has confirmed over and over again each time I have someone tell their story, cry, or just find something beautiful about themselves. I began to see this is my ministry. Every time I enter someone's closet it is sacred space to listen, love, and learn. I am doing His work for His glory.

As I read these testimonials, it occurs to me that having Christians working in fashion could be the only way to reach some very hurt people. Maybe some industries need Christians working in them the most?

Take my friend Jamie, who was a bartender during college. When people asked her how a Christian could possibly feel okay working in a bar, she would ask them: Who would you rather have serving your young son or daughter who doesn't yet know their limit? She relished the responsibility of taking care of people, sometimes comforting them in their lowest moments.

No matter your vocation, I believe that God can and will use that to spread His kingdom if you're open to it. In his book *Meaning at the Movies: Becoming a Discerning Viewer*, Grant Horner says:

> I contend that Scripture does not call us to evacuate ourselves entirely from the pagan culture that surrounds us, but to use our wise and prudent interaction with that culture to help us grow in our appreciation of God's grace toward us, to see that what God says about fallen mankind is in fact absolutely accurate (even as found in pagan works), and to better equip us for interaction with the many human beings who do not yet know him.

In many ways, this has been the guiding principle of J's Everyday Fashion since day one. When I started in May 2010, I was on a mission to make a positive impact on fashion journalism. In an industry that I saw as often a dark place, with a heavy focus on exorbitant prices and unrealistic beauty ideals, I believed that my little website could be an uplifting force that focused on inclusion, not exclusion, where women of all budgets, ages, skin colors, body types, and disabilities felt welcome to enjoy fashion. Through the site, I aim to show God's love and His welcoming spirit within the fashion world. And when I was called (literally on the phone) to write a faith-based book, I was open to taking on that challenge and obeying that call. I now see how God could possibly use the little website I've built as a platform for His love in ways I never imagined!

Growing up in the Christian culture, I didn't have very many role models who worked in the arts. Yes, there were singers like Amy Grant, Carmen, and DC Talk, who at the height of their popularity were arguably just as fierce as their secular counterparts. And Joshua Harris was a fedora-wearing rock star on the cover of his popular book *I Kissed Dating Goodbye*. Beyond that, though, there weren't any designers or fashion icons in Christian pop culture (at least, that I knew of).

Looking back, I wonder how watching Christians in the limelight who do interior design, such as HGTV's Chip and Joanna Gaines, would've affected my outlook and journey on this question of fashion and faith. Chip and Joanna are great examples of how you can represent your Christian faith in any vocation. As stars of the popular HGTV series *Fixer Upper*, their jobs (especially Joanna's) are based in the arts, and their show is not faith-based or evangelistic; however, off air they openly share their testimony, and their faith in God is well known. (I actually believe it would have done less, potentially, to serve God's kingdom if the Gaineses had insisted that *Fixer Upper* be a faith-based show. Instead, they are like the shiplap Trojan horse of Christian values that has been sent into popular culture. They are able to do even more good work for Christ by being on a network like HGTV, spreading God's love so much wider and reaching people not otherwise possible to reach.)

In the Parable of Scattered Seed in Matthew 13, the farmer only finds success when his seeds land in fertile soil. The farmer in this parable is spreading the Good News, or evangelizing, but perhaps some of our jobs are to spread seed, while others produce the fertile soil or the culture in which those seeds are planted. That rich environment helps further the growth of the seeds, enabling them to "produce a crop [that is] a hundred, sixty, or thirty times what was sown" by the farmer (NIV).

Of course, Christian artists who've achieved a certain degree of fame are susceptible to additional criticism in some faith circles. Consider any Christian whose job inherently requires promoting herself, allowing her face and body to be used in images in magazines or on TV: a singer, an actress, a reality-show star, or a fashion blogger. Are we still promoting Christ through our work, or are we really just promoting ourselves? Fashion models' careers, for example, are completely based on their outer appearance. Their aspirations are to be photographed and for their faces and bodies to appear on the covers and pages of magazines. Are all fashion models sinning just by being models? Are Chip and Joanna sinning by participating in a TV show that makes them "famous"?

I went out to dinner with my friend Jaime recently (a different Jaime, not the bartender). Singing is Jaime's lifelong passion. While we were chatting, she asked me, "Is it wrong that I crave an audience for my craft?" I told her that while it was a question only she could answer for herself, knowing her heart, I couldn't imagine that her desire was coming from a bad place.

Perhaps Jaime was troubled by this passage, in Galatians 1:10: "Am I now trying to win the approval of human beings, or of God? Or am I trying to please people? If I were still trying to please people, I would not be a servant of Christ" (NIV).

But Jaime's desire to sing, much like my desire to be creative with clothes, comes from a very precious part of her soul. She has dreamt of singing her whole life. And she has the pipes to really *sing*, so why wouldn't she invite people to listen and enjoy her voice? If she is singing to give God glory and to spread His light (yes, even within the "secular" music industry), why wouldn't she want people to hear her? If she didn't, wouldn't it be like hiding God's light? The author Leo Buscaglia put it best: "Your talent is God's gift to you. What you do with it is your gift back to God."

The natural desire of any artist is to want to share it, and I don't believe that God wants us to hide our craft from others. Matthew 5:14–16 says:

> You are the light of the world . . . People [do not] light a lamp and put it under a bowl. Instead they put it on its stand, and it gives light to everyone in the house. In the same way, let your light shine before others, that they may see your good deeds and glorify your Father in heaven. (NIV)

If you make beautiful music like Jaime, why not share it with a crowd? If you create beautiful homes in Texas like the Gaineses, why not share them on TV? If you delight in creating new outfits, why not share them on a blog? I think it's easy to assume that anyone in the limelight is there because they wish to be famous. But more often than not they are compelled to act, to write books, to sing, or to dance because it would crush their soul not to do it. Sharing their art is the only thing that's up for negotiation, and the spirit behind that sharing has the potential to touch someone's heart and mind—to make them laugh, to help them heal, to inspire them so much that something changes, and they have a breakthrough or try something new. The desire to share our experience and talents with one another comes from a healthy place and is one of the deepest parts of our human nature.

Don't get me wrong. I can see how posting pictures of myself wearing different outfits over the years looks completely narcissistic. I have seen that criticism of fashion blogging so many times! And while it's possible that, for some, the motivation behind blogging is ego and vanity, trust me when I say it's certainly not everyone's. Blogging for me has nothing to do with wishing to be famous, or being so into myself that I want to share a million selfies. I wanted to make a difference in fashion journalism, and I'm unconcerned enough about my self-image that I'm comfortable posting pictures—even imperfect, sometimes hilarious images of me in bad outfits that can never be erased from the internet. (Never, guys. Like, never.)

Because, believe me, I know I am not a supermodel! My outside is covered in flaws, and people sometimes laugh and poke fun at them. But I live in the truth that my inner beauty is what matters, and I want to share the light of my art and creativity with the world. For me, there is so much joy in the craft itself—of making outfits and of creating content for websites, lookbooks, and magazine spreads. And it gives me a sense of deep purpose. So even if it means spreading all my flaws far and wide on the internet and knowing I may be taken for a narcissist, I'm willing to post pictures of my imperfect self. It comes with the gig. It's not my favorite part, but it's totally worth it.

Whether you consider fashion your calling in the sense that you enjoy it as a hobby, or your calling in the sense that it's your career, is of little consequence. A calling is not always your job. A calling is when something is stirred so deeply in your heart from a young age that you know you have to do it. Maybe your church tells you it's sinful to buy the color red, or maybe your parents are disapproving of your career as a hairdresser, but you still feel that urge. The desire to create for you comes from a deeper place, a longing that has whispered to you from a young age; it has little to do with impressing anyone around you or "looking pretty."

As author Leland Ryken says in *The Liberated Imagination: Thinking Christianly About the Arts*: "If artistic creativity is, as the Bible claims, a gift of God, we can scarcely demonstrate our gratitude for the gift any more adequately than by using and enjoying it." When we feel that deeper spiritual undercurrent, it is possible that we have found our calling from God, and that He is drawing us in. And nothing honors Him more than when we answer that call.

Chapter 3

Is Fashion Necessary?

Picture for a moment that it's Monday morning. You're sitting in a meeting at work, surrounded by your colleagues, and you're naked. Or you're getting up onstage to give a speech, naked. How about shopping for groceries naked? Or playing tennis naked?

Nudist colonies might be the ideal lifestyle for a select few, but for most of us, nudity is not what we signed up for. In the Garden of Eden, one of our very first tasks as humans with freedom was to cover ourselves up. Adam and Eve bit into that apple, realized they were naked, and immediately made coverings for themselves.

> When the woman saw that the fruit of the tree was good for food and pleasing to the eye, and also desirable for gaining wisdom, she took some and ate it. She also gave some to her husband, who was with her, and he ate it. Then the eyes of both of them were opened, and they realized they were naked; so they sewed fig leaves together and made coverings for themselves. (Genesis 3:67, NIV)

Have you ever seen the show *Naked and Afraid* on the Discovery Channel? The first time I saw a commercial for it, I assumed the "naked" part was a marketing ploy to get people to watch. But upon further investigation I discovered that nudity is actually an inherent part of the story (and that the show has a hefty postproduction budget so that everyone's nether regions are thoroughly pixelated).

In the show, two survivalists, a man and a woman, are dropped off in the wild with no clothes, and they have to survive for twenty-one days. The nudity provides a form of social rhetoric, and the exchange that takes place around the nakedness is fascinating. Everyone reacts differently to their partner and to themselves being naked. Some are unfazed by the nudity, and some choose to build coverings for their naked bodies. Some do so even before their most basic needs of food, water, and shelter are met.

The urgency contestants experience for covering themselves is understandable. Our clothes cover things like cellulite and body hair, which society tells us are undesirable and best kept hidden from sight. They also conceal the perhaps unflattering things a naked body does as it performs tasks, like bending over. There's an episode of *Seinfeld* in which Jerry dates a woman who likes to be naked every minute of the day. He thinks that's great at first, but he quickly learns it's just really not that attractive watching a naked person do many of the ordinary activities of daily life. Jerry ultimately ends the relationship because her affinity for being naked proves to be too much for him.

The show *Naked and Afraid* goes well beyond a study of being nude in front of the opposite sex; it's also a major reality check about the practicality of wearing clothes. One survivalist on the show steps on something sharp on the first day and almost has to have his foot amputated from the resulting infection. (Cute shoes have never seemed more important, guys!) Without clothes to protect them from the elements, contestants suffer from dangerous sunburns, hypothermia, and bug bites in places you've never imagined. And how about the hygiene factor? What would chairs and public benches be like if we didn't wear clothes? Like a cesspool of bacteria, which is pretty gross.

Truly, there is some deep utilitarian part of me that wants to do away with fashion completely. For the sake of finding peace with a topic that creates so much tension with my faith and personal values, why not just eliminate fashion altogether? Sometimes I think about how people can completely sustain from other vices, like drugs or alcohol. But the same isn't true of clothes. Clothes are, in so many ways, the essential sin. Which is, of course, a paradox—something essential can't possibly be a sin. And yet it often feels that way, doesn't it? We may feel in a religious-based setting that clothing is off-limits, while even the most conservative financial planners recommend a line item for clothing in your personal budget because clothing, at its core, is a necessity.

As clothing is so unavoidable, we must dedicate some of our resources to getting ourselves dressed each morning. So why not then draw the line there, at absolute necessity? Why not adopt a Henry David Thoreau approach and only own the bare essentials, wearing the same few items each day?

While that's certainly an option, humans like to complicate things. Whether we choose to participate in societal constructs is one thing, but there's no arguing that they exist. Every social situation we attend—whether it's a wedding, a church service, or a job interview—comes with a myriad of rules and faux pas to navigate in terms of getting dressed. Putting practicality aside, like protection from the sun, cold, germs, and bug bites, we still must face a complex and sometimes maddening labyrinth of social cues and dress-code rules. We live in a highly appearance-based society; what we wear has an impact on our own lives, as well as those around us.

How Our Clothing Identifies Us

I was twenty-one, fresh out of college, and headed to an exciting job interview. Having grown up and attended college in Kansas, I was just a couple months into my new life in Boston. I hadn't completely caught on yet that Boston is a very buttoned-up, dressy city, especially compared to the Midwest. I also had hardly any money in my bank account, exorbitant rent to pay, and a completely utilitarian outlook on fashion. So I decided not to purchase a suit or similar appropriate attire for my job interview. Not my best call.

My skills and qualifications were a perfect fit for the company and the position, and I'm a pro at interviews—I aced all my job interview tests in college, and beyond that singular experience I almost always get a call back. But when I walked in that day, in a casual skirt and jacket, I immediately sensed something was wrong. I had a sinking feeling that I really should've been wearing a suit. The atmosphere of the office was much more formal than I had expected, and I could feel the interviewer's disapproving gaze toward my outfit.

I didn't get the job that day because of how I was dressed, or rather, how my clothes identified me: sloppy, lazy, not willing to go the extra mile, and simply not caring enough about the interview to dress appropriately. It was a turning point for me. There are many instances in life where Henry David Thoreau just wasn't going to cut it. Perhaps if I were living at Walden Pond, then being utilitarian would be just fine. But dressing the part was going to be an unavoidable issue if I wanted to work in an office in a big city.

I once read an article on a popular lifestyle website about a woman who felt very strongly that she should be able to conduct speaking engagements wearing yoga pants, messy hair, and no makeup. Furthermore, she asserted, everyone should respect her the same way they would if she were wearing a suit. And you know what? I agree with her on some level. Why does our appearance matter so much? In some ways, it felt very unfair to be judged by my clothes in that job interview. It would have been a real financial risk for me to buy a suit before landing the job I needed to help pay for it—a counting-your-chickens-before-they-hatch type of situation. (Note: if you are ever in a financially difficult situation like I was and need clothes for a job interview, you may want to seek out your local Dress for Success, a nonprofit dedicated to providing professional attire to women.)

And yet, within our society, our clothing and appearance is one of the most powerful forms of nonverbal communication. What *would* we think if a guest speaker we admired showed up to his speech in pajamas? It would indubitably change our opinion of him, and perhaps cause us to (somewhat unfairly) judge everything he had say before he even opened his mouth. Certainly, life would be more fair if people looked to the heart the way that it says that God does in 1 Samuel 16:7, but unfortunately that's just not the case: "The Lord does not look at the things people look at. People look at the outward appearance, but the Lord looks at the heart" (NIV).

Clothing at the most basic level identifies who we are in life. A white collar and black robes? You're probably a priest. Unkempt hair and dirty clothes? Some may assume you are homeless. A three-piece suit and Italian leather shoes? You're probably a businessman or woman. Pajamas and no makeup? It's unlikely you're a powerful speaker at a major conference.

Stereotypes and superficial judgments can sometimes be way off or even offensive. Still, people use them—consciously or not—to quickly evaluate a person and decide how to communicate with him. Think about it. We would approach meeting a priest and a businessman differently—everything from our handshake to how we identify ourselves. And while we may adopt a gentler approach toward someone who is unkempt, we'd likely apply a more direct approach toward someone confidently wearing bright colors. Right or wrong, you are often identified largely by what you are wearing.

One of my favorite episodes of the TV show *What Not to Wear* features actress and neuroscientist Mayim Bialik. On the show, Mayim's outlook on fashion could be summarized as completely utilitarian. She wanted nothing to do with getting dressed, and she refused to participate in the subject of style, so she just threw on whatever baggy maxi skirt and T-shirt she could find rumpled up in her closet.

Her friends and family were not having it, which might seem unloving or mean at first. *Let Mayim dress however she wants!* you might be thinking. I tend to agree, because I'm all about freedom and personal expression. But in this particular case, Mayim wasn't making any style decisions *at all.* Or at least she thought she wasn't making any decisions, which was a style decision in and of itself. Her friends and family wanted her to know that the signals she was sending to the world through her clothes were "I don't care" or "I'm not well." And they knew those were not really the right signals at all—Mayim did care and she was doing just fine.

There will always be people who rebel against society's expectations when it comes to style and grooming, and honestly, I don't blame them. I often enjoy going against the status quo myself. It's just important to understand that while we can choose not to participate, we can't control or change the responses we'll receive because of that choice. We can't always expect to land the job, get a date, or even make friends in certain circles if we're not participating within certain socially accepted boundaries. And we can't walk around naked. So, on the most basic level, there will always be the question of what to wear, every single morning, and how we answer it absolutely matters.

How Our Clothing Transforms Us

In college I was elected VP of recruitment for my sorority. Part of my responsibilities included planning and running a weeklong recruitment training for the entire house, which had about 120 women, called Work

Week. Everyone was required to attend, it was a total drag, and we all hated it. In years past, our VP of recruitment would yell, scream, and overall not be very nice to us during Work Week. It was awful!

While I understood that being an authority figure would not always mean being a friend, I also really wanted to set a different tone for Work Week that year. So I concocted a plan with my assistant VP of recruitment. The morning that Work Week started, we dressed up in "coach" outfits, complete with whistles, sweatbands, and athletic gear. We waited until everyone was gathered in the dining room, and then we made our entrance like a couple of cheerleaders, blowing our whistles with tons of energy. We wanted to start things off on the right foot, with a little boost in morale and some pep in our step. We were in charge, but we were also there to have *fun*.

My reputation up until this point had been as the best-dressed girl in the house. I specifically wanted to be stripped of my "fashion crown" during Work Week so that I could come from a place of approachability. So I allowed the girls to dress me up however they wanted each day. There were some pretty goofy outfits, but the day I was wearing a tutu takes the cake. Some Panhellenic officials came to our house, and I totally forgot what I was wearing until I answered the door and saw the looks on their faces. (Try explaining that one!)

In the end it was completely worth it. Our recruitment numbers went up 40 percent that year, and I believe the uplifting tone during training helped to make it happen. My goofy clothes played well into my goofy personality. They gave me the freedom to dance around and make faces during song practice, and kept me from entering dictator territory (at least most of the time; I'm sure I wasn't the perfect leader by any means). By stripping myself of my best-dressed identity, I was able to change the perception of the VP of recruitment and get the reaction I wanted, and I enjoyed myself immensely, even during the dreaded Work Week.

In the TV series *Younger*, the main character, Liza, pushes this connection between fashion and perception even further by inventing a totally new identity for herself. Fortysomething, newly divorced, and financially strapped, she's forced to sell her house in the suburbs and go back to work in New York City for the first time in fifteen years. The only problem is that at every job interview, her age proves to be a major problem. Nobody wants a "washed-up woman in her forties" who has been out of the industry for more than a decade. So with her back against the wall, she makes a decision—why not just pretend to be in her midtwenties? And it works!

Admittedly, the actress who plays Liza (Sutton Foster) was blessed with good genes and a bit of a baby face, but what's fascinating to me is how makeup and clothes transform her character in the show. In some scenes, Liza is back in her fortysomething life. By simply putting on a pencil skirt and sensible shoes, she is "Liza, the responsible suburban mom" that plays it safe, goes to bed early, and is a bit of a bookworm. In the next scene, she's wearing a miniskirt and a beanie and she's suddenly, "Liza, the twentysomething hip young professional," who stays out late with her friends, has a hot new boyfriend, and is just starting her career. It's incredible to see what one little costume change can do.

Not only can clothing impact how other people see us, it can also impact how we see ourselves and how we behave. In a study published in the *Journal of Experimental Social Psychology* in 2012, participants were given a white coat and told that it was either a doctor's coat or a painter's coat. They were then asked to perform some basic functions of the assigned vocation while wearing the coat. The participants acted differently depending on which type of coat they thought they were wearing: "Wearing a lab coat described as a doctor's coat increased sustained attention compared to wearing a lab coat described as a painter's coat."[1]

---

1 Sandra Blakeslee, "Mind Games: Sometimes a White Coat Isn't Just a White Coat," *New York Times*, April 2, 2012, http://www.nytimes.com/2012/04/03/science/clothes-and-self-perception.html.

In other words, when the participants were told they were wearing a doctor's coat rather than a painter's coat, they took their suggested job much more seriously and acted out basic functions of each job with much greater care. We've all heard the phrase "dress for the position you want" a million times, but this study shows it truly has merit. Clothing has the ability to alter us, whether it's by stripping away our armor and allowing us to show ourselves as vulnerable, or helping us feel the part and then landing a promotion: clothing has a transformative nature that's hard to deny.

Clothing: Our Connector . . . and Divider

"That's such a cute dress!" "That color looks fabulous on you." "Cute shoes, where did you get them?" These are just a few of the phrases you might hear me say to complete strangers on any given day. I'm naturally outgoing and love meeting new people and connecting with women anywhere—whether it's at a networking event or simply strolling down the grocery-store aisle. Given my love for fashion, I am apt to make a comment or give a compliment to open the door to getting to know someone better.

In some situations, like a work conference, my opening line may switch to a more industry-focused question, like, "Who are some of your current clients?" or "How long have you been in this field?" If I spot someone in a colorful outfit or cute shoes that speaks to my soul, though, I'm likely to open that door and make a connection over fashion, because it's something near and dear to my heart.

For some, this type of compliment can feel like a shallow focus on appearance. Or it may feed the notion that we are pressuring each other as women, or setting up expectations to look a certain way. And I hear that, I really do. But at the end of the day, who doesn't appreciate a compliment? I love speaking positivity to other people! And ultimately there's not much to go on if you haven't spoken to them yet—a fashion compliment is an obvious icebreaker that can easily turn into deeper questions and conversations.

It's not only women like me who connect with other women through fashion small talk, though. I have guy friends who have met people simply because they were wearing a Syracuse shirt, and my friends stopped to talk to them about sports. I once wore a Kansas City Royals T-shirt to watch the World Series on a cruise ship, and I met every person in the room because they were curious about my shirt.

Consider that recent commercial for Pandora jewelry. A woman is attending a party with her husband, where she meets his boss's wife. Within seconds, she knows intimate details about her—that she loves the beach, she's been to London and Paris, and her son plays baseball. The woman's husband gasps, thinking that she must be psychic (meanwhile, the rest of us just assume she's really good at Facebook stalking). But no, she just "speaks Pandora," meaning she observed the charms on the boss's wife's bracelet. When fashion tells your whole life story without your ever opening your mouth, it certainly makes it easier to connect.

While I'm all about celebrating the positive side of fashion, and the transformative and connective power it brings to the table, I would be remiss not to mention the darker side as well, and the way in which it sometimes tears us apart. You may be saying to yourself right now, "Pump the brakes! Is this chick seriously telling us we need to conform to a bunch of rules set forth by society on what we wear and how we look?" To which I would reply, "I like your fortitude. Keep that up. And allow me to clarify: I'm not onboard with some of the requirements society puts forth to look a certain way, particularly as they apply to women."

Two sociologists, Jaclyn Wong of the University of Chicago and Andrew Penner of the University of California at Irvine, studied 14,000 people over the course of several years to see how physical attractiveness relates to income. Their findings, published in the June 2016 issue of the journal *Research in Social Stratification and Mobility*, state that "attractive" individuals earn up to 20 percent more than others.[2] And it turns out that "attractive" doesn't just refer to the kind of beauty you're born with, but also to things like whether or not you wear makeup. The research showed that "well-groomed" women make $6,000 more per year, and that women who wear makeup are hired more often, get better performance reviews, and are more likely to be promoted.[3] (What?!)

One of the most striking real-life examples of this comes from the murder trial of O.J. Simpson, "the trial of the century." I was a child when the trial took place, so I don't remember firsthand much about it as it was unfolding, but I have since become fascinated with it, and specifically with lead prosecutor Marcia Clark.

Marcia Clark, as she is portrayed in *The People v. O.J. Simpson: American Crime Story*, was a powerful attorney. She had risen up the ranks in the L.A. County District Attorney's office and was a recently divorced single mom to two young boys. What I like about Marcia Clark is that she was ambitious, hardworking, and tough as nails. She didn't take flak from anyone, and she worked hard to achieve the position she was in. She also had a softer side and was a loving mom to her boys at home. She cared deeply about Nicole Brown and bringing her murderer to justice, as she had done for past victims (for example, she had successfully sent the obsessed stalker who killed actress Rebecca Schaeffer to prison for life in 1991).

Marcia Clark seems to me like a woman we would want our daughters to look up to. But as her story unfolded I was shocked to find that

---

2   Bria Balliet, "A Thing of Beauty?," UCI School of Social Sciences, May 31, 2016, http://www.socsci.uci.edu/newsevents/news/2016/2016-05-31 -penner-wong-gender.php.

3   Valentina Zarya, "How a Little Lipstick Could Add Thousands to Your Paycheck," *Fortune*, May 19, 2016, http://fortune.com/2016/05/19 /makeup-more-money.

she didn't become a role model for one very ridiculous reason: her hair. Our nation was obsessed with hating Marcia's hair. Mocked endlessly on the covers of magazines, spoofed on *Saturday Night Live*, and even ridiculed in the courtroom by opposing counsel, her hair was a subject everyone was talking about. Her *hair*. I am dumbfounded just thinking about how shortsighted that is.

Marcia lost the case against O.J. Simpson's legal team, despite a tremendous amount of physical evidence against Simpson. There were many contributing factors, but based on public polls in which people said they thought Marcia Clark was too "hard" and not feminine enough, is it possible that something as off-topic as hair could have influenced a jury to let a murderer walk free? No matter your beliefs about O.J.'s innocence, how crazy is that?

Recently, reports about how much money Hillary Clinton spent on clothes for her presidential campaign hit the news and were covered by the New York Post and CNBC, among others, and I kept thinking, *Would anyone ever write this about a man?* Clinton spent an astonishing $200,000-plus on her wardrobe[4] and wore a $12,495 Giorgio Armani tweed blazer for a speech in New York[5], but why is this only being reported about a woman? How much did her male counterparts spend? It could easily have been more. And would a male lawyer involved in the O.J. Simpson case ever be criticized for his potbelly or receding hairline during the "trial of a century" the way Marcia Clark's appearance was?

We don't just do this to high-profile women. On a granular level, we're advised by women's magazines that when we get married we should be careful not to "let ourselves go" and should dress up for

---

4   Leah Bourne, "The Surprising Strategy Behind Hillary Clinton's Designer Wardrobe," *New York Post*, June 5, 2016, http://nypost.com/2016/06/05/hillarys-extravagant-campaign-wardrobe-costs-at-least-200k.

5   Sarah Whitten, "This Is Why Hillary Clinton Wore a $12,000 Armani Jacket," CNBC, June 9, 2016, http://www.cnbc.com/2016/06/09/this-is-why-hillary-clinton-wore-a-12000-armani-jacket.html.

our husbands and take care of ourselves. They seem quick to tell us that every part of us needs improving, whether it's new clothes, a new hairstyle, or a new workout plan. As female editors and writers constantly send these things to press, I have to wonder, *Why do we do this to each other?*

Misogyny, to me, sometimes feels like a bucket of crabs. When you throw live crabs in a bucket, you don't need a structure over the top to contain them. Because as each crab tries to crawl out, just as they near the top, one of the other crabs will reach up and pull them back in. For hours they go on like this. Freedom is theirs for the taking, but they keep themselves in that bucket, never allowing anyone to rise to the top.

I believe that we can all contribute to changing the expectations, roles, and rules that society ingrains in us as we grow up. We can be the larger change and the difference. I would have wanted nothing more than to have seen Marcia Clark sashay into that courtroom with an amazing hairdo and throw that misogyny right back in the faces of the very people who were subjecting her to it.

But in some ways, is that surrendering?

Yes, it may be. In the eyes of many, Marcia Clark got it "wrong" with her hair. Maybe she loved her hair, and everyone should have just let her express herself however she wanted. Or maybe she didn't love it but was busy preparing for the trial of the century and didn't think something superficial like her appearance would matter so much. I can't really say. But I do know this: if we want to win, sometimes we have to play the game (not just fight to change it). We can work to change the rules in the long term (by pushing fashion and beauty boundaries and advocating for a focus on the whole person), but in the short term, we can't ignore the weight society places on appearances.

No matter your opinion on how much we should play into society's expectations, we can undoubtedly agree that clothing and beauty is an important formative force in our lives, a necessity that we should recognize and be aware of, and a transformative power within society that both connects and divides us. In the next two chapters, we'll explore this topic further as we strive to understand and utilize clothing and beauty in positive ways.

Chapter 4

Where Does Beauty Come From?

I can recall at a very young age wanting to be courted the way King Solomon courted his bride in Song of Songs. I dreamt of romance and adventure, living out those desires vicariously through my favorite princes and princesses in Disney movies. My Barbie doll and my G.I. Joe were in an illicit romance, even before I understood what that meant. For many of us, the desire to be found beautiful is inherent, put in our hearts at a very young age, and surfaces throughout our lives. It is as an essential part of our human experience—and has been throughout the ages. In Song of Songs 4, the ancient King Solomon lyrically muses:

> How beautiful you are, my darling!
> Oh, how beautiful!
> Your eyes behind your veil are doves. . . .
>
> Your hair is like a flock of goats
> descending from the hills of Gilead. . . .
>
> Your lips are like a scarlet ribbon;
> your mouth is lovely.

Your temples behind your veil
are like the halves of a pomegranate.

Your neck is like the tower of David,
built with courses of stone . . .

Your breasts are like two fawns,
like twin fawns of a gazelle
that browse among the lilies. . . .

You are altogether beautiful, my darling;
there is no flaw in you. . . .

You have stolen my heart, my sister, my bride;
you have stolen my heart

with one glance of your eyes,
with one jewel of your necklace.

How delightful is your love, my sister, my bride!

How much more pleasing is your love than wine,
and the fragrance of your perfume more than any
spice!

Your lips drop sweetness as the honeycomb, my
bride; milk and honey are under your tongue.

The fragrance of your garments is like the fragrance
of Lebanon.

You are a garden locked up, my sister, my bride;
you are a spring enclosed, a sealed fountain. . . .

You are a garden fountain, a well of flowing water
streaming down from Lebanon. (NIV)

By the time I was in my early twenties, two other pieces of writing had a strong influence on my view of our desire for beauty, *The Sacred Romance: Drawing Closer to the Heart of God* and *Wild at Heart: Discovering the Secret of a Man's Soul*, both by John Eldredge. Eldredge sets forth in his books what is to me the guiding principle when it comes to beauty and a woman's heart. He says that "the deep cry of a little girl's heart is, *Am I lovely?*"[1] Although Eldredge is gender-specific, I am confident that many of us—women and men alike—were born with an innate longing to answer this question. As Eldredge puts it, "Every woman needs to know that she is exquisite and exotic and chosen."

I've had glimpses of what that kind of beauty feels like, and perhaps you have too. Those nights when you're all dressed up for the big dance or a wedding. Your hair has somehow fallen in just the right place. Your makeup has never looked better. And that dress! You don't recall it ever looking that good in the fitting room, but in this moment you feel a bit like Cinderella. It's a magical feeling when our outer beauty comes together in this way, a feeling we were made to enjoy.

In Ezekiel 16:10–14, God metaphorically describes Jerusalem as a woman, during a time when He found the nation of Israel favorable. Can you imagine your romance playing out this way, and what splendor from God "making your beauty perfect" must feel like? It's a wonderful, delightful thought.

---

1 John Eldredge, *The Ransomed Heart: A Collection of Devotional Readings* (Nashville: Thomas Nelson, 2000), 257.

I clothed you with an embroidered dress and put sandals of fine leather on you. I dressed you in fine linen and covered you with costly garments. I adorned you with jewelry: I put bracelets on your arms and a necklace around your neck, and I put a ring on your nose, earrings on your ears and a beautiful crown on your head. So you were adorned with gold and silver; your clothes were of fine linen and costly fabric and embroidered cloth. Your food was honey, olive oil and the finest flour. You became very beautiful and rose to be a queen. And your fame spread among the nations on account of your beauty, because the splendor I had given you made your beauty perfect, declares the Sovereign Lord. (NIV)

This inherent and natural longing to feel beautiful, which is so precious and dear, unfortunately also has a dark side. In the very next line, we learn that this pure, perfect beauty did not last very long: "But you trusted in your beauty and used your fame to become a prostitute." The Enemy hits us where it hurts—over and over again—by making us question our own beauty, nudging us to strive for it in sinful ways, not from an innocent outflowing of our hearts, but from a place of vanity, ego, or greed. Everywhere we turn, messaging that plays into our insecurities is served up to us on a silver platter. The world says, "You aren't lovely, so you need this product," or, "You need to fix this about yourself, so that people will find you lovely."

Beauty, as the world presents it, is an absolute rat race. We are told that with just enough exercise, skin cream, makeup, and the right clothes and hair color, we can be the perfect woman. When we start to achieve success in one section, we start failing in another. Round and round we go, trying to keep all the plates spinning in the air, in perfect unison. We are fruitlessly hoping that one day we can achieve the desire of our hearts and answer with finality that we are lovely indeed. However, it never quite pans out that way, does it? Even if we feel we have reached that place of "perfect beauty" and things are going right for once, it never lasts; it fades, a house built on sand that's impossible to keep up.

In the previous chapter, we explored the relationship between clothes and the world around us. In this chapter, we're taking that reflection inward and removing the clothing altogether. Because in order to have a healthy relationship with clothes, I think we have to tackle the issue of loving our inner beauty first. How do we feel when we strip away the clothing, hair, and makeup, and expose our soul? How can we know for sure, in our heart of hearts, that we are lovely? And when does beauty cross the line from the healthy desire of any woman's heart to a sinful pursuit of vanity?

When We Struggle to Love Our Body

Taryn hated the way her body looked after having kids. She writes:

> I'd often stare at myself in the mirror saying, "You're fat. You are ugly. You are disgusting." I hated my body so much; I was even booked in for surgery to finally get rid of my "teabag boobs" and "hotdog roll of a tummy.[2]

Stacey struggled with rosacea. The persistent redness, bumps and pimples, and visible blood vessels that covered her face were a source of daily stress and made her struggle with the question of her own beauty.

---

2   Taryn Brumfitt, *Body Image Movement* (blog), accessed June 11, 2017, https://bodyimagemovement.com.

With rosacea she didn't feel like herself; she struggled to feel beautiful when she looked in the mirror.

When Crystal started noticing signs of aging in her thirties, she was not onboard and hated having her photos taken. She says, "When I looked at a photo of myself, all I saw was wrinkles, deflated lips, and gray hair."

My own struggle with beauty stems from the aftermath of my surgeries as a child. As I shared in chapter 1, I survived malignant tumors at the ages of three and five. I underwent extensive procedures to save my life, and the surgeries left me with an ugly scar that encircles the left side of my neck and a condition known as Horner's Syndrome, which permanently affects the symmetry of my face and eyes. Because of Horner's Syndrome, one of my eyes is brown, and the other is green. I do not sweat on the left side of my head. The pupil in my left eye stays small at all times, and my left eyelid droops.

The first three symptoms of Horner's I can handle. Having two different eye colors makes for a great conversation starter. Sweating on only one side of my face means that my hair and makeup on the other side always look perfect, even after the gym or on a hot summer day. And my pupil staying small has a very little, if any, effect on my vision. But my eyelid drooping? Ouch. That one hurts. Nothing has affected my struggle to feel beautiful more than my left eye.

Why does my eyelid cause me so much more grief than the other symptoms of Homer's Syndrome? Because it's been scientifically proven that symmetry equals attractiveness.[3] There have been numerous studies in which participants rate people's attractiveness, and those with the highest scores have symmetrical faces. Tom Cruise and Elizabeth Hurley, for example, are found to have perfectly symmetrical faces, which is one

---

3   Charles Feng, "Looking Good: The Psychology and Biology of Beauty," *Journal of Young Investigators* 6, no 6 (December 2002). http://legacy.jyi .org/volumes/volume6/issue6/features/feng.html.

of the reasons why people rate them as very attractive. Even in nature, female birds show preference for males with more symmetrical tails or colored leg bands. The birds look for those traits because they indicate a healthy diet and a lack of genetic defects and disease, which translates to a better chance of healthy offspring. People do the same thing. It's in our nature to find the perfectly symmetrical more attractive, as we look for a mate that will help us produce healthy offspring. In other words, people are genetically programmed to not find me attractive, and I was programmed to not feel attractive. Thank you, nature.

I'm a huge advocate for loving the skin we're in. I speak about it often on my blog—I believe that every skin color, body type, disability, and skin condition, as well as gray hairs, wrinkles, and postkid bodies, should be represented and respected in the media. I believe that the things that make us different, like our scars and our idiosyncrasies, are truly what make us beautiful. I don't accept society's definition that only supermodels with specific measurements are the sole representation of attractiveness.

Of course, while I'm a champion for other women's belief in their own beauty and encourage them to love the skin they're in, I struggle when I turn those notions inward. It's a challenge for me to live out these beliefs fully in my own everyday life. I have moments of doubt. I nitpick at my body and appearance.

And I'm not alone. Stacy decided to invest in expensive skin treatments to cure her rosacea, and Crystal got Botox and lip fillers and dyed her gray hair to combat the signs of aging. Taryn, on the other hand, canceled her plastic surgery, deciding that it was not her body that needed to change, but her attitude toward it. When it came to my eyelid, I didn't take Taryn's route. At the age of nineteen, I opted to have plastic surgery. (Before that surgery, my case of Horner's Syndrome was so bad that my eyelid, especially when I didn't get enough sleep, was almost completely closed.) Opting to have this procedure is a decision I still contemplate today. How will I explain my reasoning to any future children I'm blessed with? Because when, if ever, is it okay to take action and change our outer appearance with surgery, skin treatments, and antiaging remedies, and when is it not? And how do we finally find that place of unconditionally loving the body and the skin that we are in?

Drawing the (Beauty) Line

Prior to college, I didn't have any hang-ups about my drooping eyelid. No one ever commented on it at my small Christian high school, and I never really noticed the asymmetry of my face. But when I entered a large public university, the remarks began. A girl left a message mocking my "lazy eye" on the white board that hung on my dorm room door. (People often referred to it as a lazy eye, even though that's a different condition.) Another time, a boy I'd broken up with had his friends leave me a mocking voicemail about my eye. And strangers in public were regularly asking, "Hey, what's wrong with your eye?" I had not experienced much shame about myself until that point, but these experiences caught me up to speed quickly, and I found myself wallowing in it. I didn't just feel slightly unattractive, I felt like Quasimodo, the king of all outsiders.

I remembered my doctor mentioning that eyelid surgery would be possible once I was eighteen, so I sprang into action. I asked my mom to take me to a specialist who could administer tests and appeal to our health insurance to cover the surgery. The tests proved that my peripheral vision was adversely affected by my drooping eyelid, and insurance approved the surgery. I still had one big hurdle, though—asking my dad to cover the deductible, which was something like a thousand dollars. No small task in my family, and I absolutely hated to do it. Outer appearances were not important in our family culture, and even asking for a new pair of jeans would generally be turned down. But I was so determined and wanted the surgery so badly that I mustered up the courage, and with enough (very genuine) tears and begging, my dad agreed to cover the cost.

The surgery was quick. It was a day of intense pain, and then my eyelid healed quickly, with no scarring. The results were not as I had hoped, though. Because now, instead of drooping from Horner's, my eyelid was unnaturally propped open from plastic surgery. As I would come to find out, there is no perfect fix for a drooping eyelid. My eyes will always and forever be a different shape and size from one another. The surgery improved the drooping immensely, but my left eye is still nowhere near perfect.

After my eyelid surgery, I also realized that I still felt the same inside as I had before. My outer appearance may have been somewhat "corrected," but my heart and mind still had some catching up to do. I felt like the same girl who had been teased, and I was still more focused on my appearance than I should've been. Even years after surgery, I actually believed at one point that my eyelid was a barrier to my being a successful blogger. I was about twenty-seven and had recently started my blog, and I remember several long conversations with friends on the topic. I was stuck on this idea that no one would ever put someone who looked like me in a magazine or on TV, so why should I foolishly put photos of myself on a blog?

It was mostly out of rebellion that I kept blogging—because I passionately believe that imperfect women should be in the media. It seems silly now, because lots of people have put me in magazines and on TV, and no one has ever mentioned my "imperfect" eyelid in a professional context. I know people see it—I've had plenty of unkind comments left on my blog—and I know logistically at some point I could be turned down for a project or sponsorship because of my eye, or possibly have been in the past. But I can't help but feel that the reason behind my asymmetrical face is a pretty incredible story of survival, right? Without it, I wouldn't be here today! It's my battle wound, and I have become incredibly proud of what it symbolizes.

I'm also thankful for the inside transformation I've experienced—the teasing gave me character and a heart for others who feel marginalized and like outcasts because of their appearance. I believe it has contributed greatly to my career choice and decision to dedicate my life to putting "everyday women" in the media. I am thankful that I don't live under the impression that I could ever look perfect, or that I would ever think too highly of or put too much faith in my looks. Searching for perfect outer beauty is not only an impossible task, but it also can be an exhausting pursuit and a slippery slope.

But wait one minute, you might be saying. Wasn't my decision to fix my eyelid already encroaching on the sin of vanity? And, as a woman of faith, aren't there very important reasons to eschew any attempt at perfect beauty? Because in many religious sects, plastic surgery of any kind, or even wearing makeup, is frowned upon or forbidden, and my decision to choose plastic surgery could very easily be labeled a sin. And while many of us may think that it's natural for Stacey to treat her rosacea and Crystal to color her gray hairs, others believe they shouldn't alter themselves at all. This year the gray hairs have started popping up all over my head like unwelcome prairie dogs, but part of me questions why are they "unwelcome" in the first place? I have yet to cover the grays or purchase an "antiwrinkle" cream, because is there really a reason to be anti wrinkles at all? I might actually be pro "my face," every last bit of it.

The other side of the argument presents questions too, like: Why not keep your outer appearance and "beauty" intact and looking great? Why not opt for Botox if it makes you feel infinitely better, is not unreasonable for your financial situation, and is not harming yourself or others? If there's an opportunity to feel great in photos again, why not take it? Where's the sin in that? I may be inclined to agree, but where exactly do we draw the line?

I will never forget the episode of the TLC series *My Strange Addiction* about Lacey Wildd that I watched years ago. I think most would say that Lacey is an example of a person who's moved beyond harmless, superficial changes to a controlling preoccupation with physical appearance. She has gone from an A-cup to a QQQ as the result of twelve breast augmentation surgeries. Her breasts weigh forty-two pounds; to support the weight she had pigskin sewn inside her abdomen. On the show, she talks about the dangers of having large breasts: everything from knocking her young daughter over to accidentally burning them on the stove while she cooks. Her six children plead with her to stop. Her daughter sullenly confesses, "My life revolves around her boobs," and yet Lacey presses on, in search of her next procedure and the "perfect" body.

It can be easy to identify Lacey Wildd, who has an actual addiction and is causing harm to herself and others, as crossing the line. But other times, crossing the line is sneakier, and it's harder to diagnose. We may not consider Stacey's treatment of her rosacea as revolutionary, but that night at her Bible study, the women in her group dug deeper to get to the root of the problem. Stacey broke down crying, because she realized her rosacea was making her question her beauty on a much deeper level. Her skin problem had an actual hold over her spiritual life and was preventing her from seeing herself as God sees her. The skin creams and remedies may have been perfectly acceptable (at least, compared to multiple rounds of extreme surgeries), but what lies underneath and the issues of her heart were just as important and urgent to address as those plaguing Lacey Wildd.

So how do we identify when we have crossed this line for ourselves? (Because, at times, it certainly feels as gray as the hairs on my head.)

Breaking things down into the following areas of concern helps me bring it into focus:

The amount of time we spend. When we spend such an exorbitant amount of time on our outer appearance that it keeps us from focusing on more important things like our health, relationships, or career.

The amount of money we spend. When we spend such an excessive amount of money on our outer appearance that it damages our overall financial well-being.

The disapproval of family/friends. When our pursuit for the perfect outer appearance becomes a point of dissension with our family and friends and puts pressure on or ends important relationships.

Our own safety. When our pursuit of outer beauty is dangerous or high-risk, or leads us to put our bodies through physical harm.

Our state of mind. When we feel we can't live without altering our outer appearance, or our outer appearance is being used to mask a much deeper or bigger problem.

Using Aristotle's *On Virtues and Vices* as our guide, there are two ends of any spectrum, and the extreme nature of either end is not good. On one end of the beauty spectrum we have "vanity," or the pursuit of outer appearance in an unhealthy or extreme way. On the other end, we have "pusillanimous," which is defined by *Merriam-Webster's* as "lacking courage and resolution, marked by contemptible timidity." (In other words, you care so little about your outer appearance that it's also a problem.)

Aristotle does not go into detail about how this spectrum works in terms of self-love, but I am willing to theorize that on either end of the spectrum lies self-hate. When you are too much into altering your appearance that it becomes an unhealthy endeavor, at the core lies a dissatisfaction with your beauty. On the opposite end, when you are so uninterested in your outer appearance that you dangerously gain weight or ignore your hygiene, then you also have a deep dissatisfaction with your beauty or could be struggling with low self-esteem.

In the middle, in the gray area, is where we actually find self-love. Which is good news—because most of us are out there in the gray area, trying to navigate the murky waters and find a healthy balance in our exercise routines, skin treatments, and hair-dyeing.

But how often are the little decisions to "do something" about our external appearance—from pushing ourselves to lose weight to investing in acne treatments—about something much deeper? When this happens, how can we identify the internal struggle at play, and how do we finally resolve the question of our beauty once and for all?

True Beauty: What God Sees

The easiest way to love our bodies is often by recognizing their scientific or practical values. We may marvel at our ability to birth children, to run marathons, or to swim laps. Anyone who has beat cancer or gone through a prolonged illness knows the feeling of being thankful for the ability to walk, sing, and dance. And while we may easily love our bodies because of our good health, seeing it as a beautiful thing to behold, especially in the eyes of the opposite sex, can be a losing battle or just simply makes us laugh. And when things like an injury, a blemish, or weight gain happen, we might struggle to hold onto that thankfulness and start to see our bodies as the enemy. We may admire our bodies on a deeper level, but calling ourselves lovely, desirable, and an object of infinite beauty? That's an entirely different challenge altogether, and many of us to struggle to see our bodies that way (myself included).

How can we settle the issue of beauty and answer the cry of our heart (*Am I lovely?*)? First and foremost, we must understand the true nature and source of our beauty. That's the biggest piece of the puzzle— knowing and believing that our beauty comes from our Creator.

Genesis 1:27 says that we were made in His image, and as bearers of His image, we are infinitely beautiful. We can rest in the knowledge that He, the most beautiful masterpiece of all, is the foundation from which all our beauty (internal and external) flows. "So God created mankind in his own image, in the image of God He created them; male and female He created them." (NASB)

We see another example of our inherent beauty in the baptism of Jesus in Matthew 3:17: "And suddenly a voice came from heaven saying, 'This is My beloved Son, in whom I am well pleased'" (NKJV). It's important to note that this pronouncement and praise was given before Jesus performed any of the miracles or healings that He is so well known for. In other words, God is already pleased, before we've ever "earned" it, and being inherently beloved means God is already pleased with us!

Another important part of understanding our beauty is determining who defines our beauty. The media, your coworkers or classmates, and strangers on social media—these are people who may judge you based on your external attributes, giving little thought to your heart and mind. But while they may solely be focused on your outer appearance, that's not what God sees. Straight from His mouth, appearances are not what's He's after. He's after your heart, dear girl. It's up to us to decide if it's His approval we are after, or someone else's.

> But the Lord said to Samuel, "Do not consider his appearance or his height, for I have rejected him. The Lord does not look at the things people look at. People look at the outward appearance, but the Lord looks at the heart." (1 Samuel 16:7, NIV)

When we accept God as the judge of our beauty and we dig deeper, we learn more from His word on how he defines beauty. In 1 Peter 3:3–4, Jesus says that our beauty is "that of our inner self, the unfading beauty of a gentle and quiet spirit, which is of great worth in God's sight" (NIV). He makes it clear that our beauty is not about our outer appearances at all. He's okay with the outer adornments—after all, those things can be our art and a precious form of expression of worship to Him. However, they are not the *source* of our beauty and God's not like other people who may judge us by our outer appearance—that's simply not how He judges us at all. God's definition of beauty is what your well-meaning grandmother once said: it's what's on the inside that counts.

We've all heard it. Probably when a loved one or friend was trying to soothe our hurt feelings after we were rejected by a boy or made fun of at school, and we probably rolled our eyes as hard as we could. But it's actually true; the source of our beauty is our heart! And when we finally grasp this concept and accept it as truth, we can begin to transform, releasing any dependence on outward appearances and truly living in the belief that beauty comes from our hearts and minds.

In *Becoming Myself: Embracing God's Dream of You*, Stasi Eldredge says:

> Beauty is not about the hair, the clothes . . . or the number on the scale. Being beautiful is a quality of spirit recognized primarily in a woman whose soul is at rest because she believes her God when he calls her lovely. She is no longer striving to reach the world's unattainable standards of beauty and acceptance but instead is receiving her inheritance that is hers as an image bearer of the living God. She is embracing who God made her to be.[4]

---

4 Stasi Eldredge, *Beautiful Now: 90 Days of Experiencing God's Dreams for You* (Colorado Springs, CO: David C. Cook, 2016).

A couple years ago I gained weight due to some medical issues, enough to move me up one or two clothing sizes. If magazine covers are to be believed, a weight-gain situation generally calls for some serious alarm bells. Certainly, I should be doing something drastic to get back into my old clothing. While it was frustrating not being able to wear some of my favorite clothes, I also refused to buy into the belief that something was "wrong" or that I couldn't be beautiful at any size. What would that say about the other women who were my new larger size? Certainly they all looked beautiful! And if my beauty is truly on the inside, then I certainly should live out that belief by not shaming myself or taking drastic measures to lose the weight.

So I did the unthinkable—at my heaviest, I proudly wore a swimsuit on vacation and even posted a picture of me jumping joyously in that swimsuit. It may not look like much to anyone else—in fact, I'm sure someone thought I was showing off my physique with that picture, because let's be real here, ladies: that body you are hating on is someone else's goal body, which means it's not fair for you to be hating on it in the first place. I didn't proclaim in the caption that I had gained weight and was doing it to be rebellious. I just posted it. Owned it. Figured someone would notice the extra padding, but I really didn't care enough to mention it. I am dedicated to living my life walking in the beauty that is defined by what's inside me, and some extra padding is of little consequence. As J. K. Rowling once said, "Is 'fat' really the worst thing a human being can be? Is 'fat' really worse than 'vindictive,' 'jealous,' 'shallow,' 'vain,' 'boring,' 'evil,' or 'cruel'? Not to me."[5]

Monica Russell, the founder of the online boutique Albanita, illustrates a real-life example of learning to believe and live in God's true source and definition of beauty. She says, "I grew up in Chicago and always loved fashion. I was really into having the hottest brands and

---

5   "JK Hits Back at 'Fat' Claims," DailyMail.com, May 12, 2006, http://www.dailymail.co.uk/tvshowbiz/article-385961/JK-hits-fat-claims.html.

trends, and being friends with the popular girls that dressed cool is where I got my confidence. I judged myself and others solely based on their outward appearance."

All of that changed when her now-husband invited her to church. Her time there pushed her further into a relationship with God. She started feeling conflicted about the way she judged her and other people's outward appearances, and came to a new understanding about the definition of true beauty. She says:

> Learning of God's faithful and endless love for me regardless of how I looked took a huge weight off of my shoulders. I started seeing other people the way God sees them, for their heart. It's so beautiful to know that it does not matter what we wear or look like, but that God sees us as precious regardless! Knowing and understanding the verse in 1 Peter 3 today, I knew I could sell clothing and accessories with a clear conscience and a pure intent. Having a grasp on inner beauty, it isn't just about selling clothing for me now, it's about helping women feel good from the inside out. I know at the end of the day God does not care what we wear, but he does care about how we feel inside and how we treat others.

When we think about beauty, we often think of all the ways we can improve our outer appearance, but when we commit to letting God define our beauty, we find that His definition is quite different. He challenges us to commit to inner beauty and be in pursuit of a godly character and the fruits of the spirit, which are "love, joy, peace, forbearance, kindness, goodness, faithfulness, gentleness and self-control" (Galatians 5:22–23, NIV).

One of the reasons God encourages us to not let our outside appearance define us is because of its shaky, impermanent nature. God challenges us to focus on inner beauty for one very simple reason: it's what lasts. Sometimes I like to believe that "losing your looks" is another ploy by marketers to get us to buy things, but God also warns us of this in Proverbs 31:30, saying, "Charm is deceptive, and beauty is fleeting; but a woman who fears the Lord is to be praised" (NIV).

I believe that aging has incredible benefits, and it's a privilege denied to many. But it also comes with challenges that even God cares to point out. Whenever I see a new gray hair pop up, I like to imagine it's a message from Him to stay focused on what matters: on our internal beauty, mind, and character.

Professional model Laura says:

> One of the myths of being beautiful is that with it, you can have it all. Yet some of the most beautiful women in the world are the most insecure. Beauty may bring a type of security, but it is an artificial security where you are building on something temporary that will fade. If that's all you have and you build your life around it, it can come crashing down very easily.[6]

Getting straight with what's underneath the clothes is an important part of our fashion journey. Believing we are made in God's image, giving God the power to define our beauty, and following His word for manifesting beauty are steps that can lead us toward settling the question of our beauty for good. When we focus on our outer appearance too much, we are in danger of missing the big picture and the meaning of life altogether. But when we can rest in this knowledge and deeper

---

6 "Life Portraits: Laura," *Models for Christ*, accessed June 11, 2017, http://www.modelsforchrist.com.

understanding of our beauty, then the control or stronghold that our outer appearance once had loses its grip, and we find we are free.

Learning to love the package that is our body, as well as the true gift of inner beauty within, is only one part of the equation, because we still must determine what to wrap it in. In the next chapter, we'll explore the ways in which our clothing, hair, and makeup affect our self-esteem, self-worth, and confidence, adding another layer to our beauty, both inside and out.

Chapter 5

How Are Fashion and Beauty Related?

When Sarah was sixteen, she went through a brutal breakup. Her long-time boyfriend suddenly and unexpectedly ended their relationship, and, to make things worse, he already had a new girlfriend. Like something straight out of a teen movie, there was a big party that night and Sarah's ex and his new girlfriend were expected to show up. Feeling rejected and humiliated, she thought, *There is no way I'm going to that party.*

Thankfully, she had my friend Melissa for a sister. Melissa is eight years older than Sarah, so she'd been out of high school long enough to possess some useful wisdom, but not so long that she couldn't fully recall how excruciating social situations like this one could be. Melissa became Sarah's fairy godmother that night, completely transforming her outer appearance with clothes and makeup. They went to the mall and bought Sarah a new outfit, and Melissa did her hair and makeup. Sarah had never felt more beautiful.

Melissa didn't stop there, though. She explained to Sarah that in this particular situation, her clothes and makeup were her armor. Using them as a shield in this situation, she informed Sarah that she was, in fact, going to do the unimaginable. The minute her ex and his new girlfriend walked in the door, she was not going to slump and hide in the corner. She was going to walk right up to them, reach out her hand, and confidently say, "Hi, I'm Sarah."

The plan worked perfectly. With her newfound confidence from her outer armor, Sarah walked right up to her ex and his new girlfriend and introduced herself. In a situation so many of us would've run from or avoided altogether, Sarah used her armor to handle it with grace and class.

In the last chapter, we talked about what our journey of fashion and faith looks like when we completely strip away the clothing, hair, and makeup. We talked about defining beauty the way that God defines it, and understanding and walking in His truth. Our inner beauty is the first layer, the precious gift that lies inside. Our second layer of beauty is the body and skin that houses our gift. This chapter is about our third layer of beauty, which is what we wrap both our inner beauty and our physical body with: clothing, hairstyles, and makeup. It is the wrapping of our gift, literally and figuratively.

The relationship between fashion and faith can be a very personal one. Our gift wrap can affect our self-image, our self-esteem, and the deepest longing of our hearts. There is a transformation that happens when we put on clothes, hair, and makeup. Sometimes that can be a source of stress; other times it can be a source of strength. When used properly, it can be downright magical. When abused, it can lead to shallowness of spirit and vanity. When have we crossed that line? And how do we balance a natural inclination and joy in decorating our external selves with the deeper understanding of how clothing and makeup relates to our inner beauty, and what truly matters?

When Clothing Is Our Superpower

When I first started college, I was painfully shy. However, I quickly discovered that a great outfit could provide me with a much-needed crutch. I felt invincible when I had confidence in my outer appearance. I went from being crippled with shyness in social situations to being able to talk to people. It was the extra little boost I needed.

We talked in chapter 3 about how a change of clothing can mean a change in vocation, social status, or position in life, by communicating a new message to those around us. In my and Sarah's scenarios, we were able to communicate something to ourselves with our clothes. Our third layer can at times contribute to our internal dialogue about our first two layers: our beauty and our body. We may not always have our source of inner beauty or our body's beauty all figured out. For many, it's a lifelong journey to write the true definition of beauty on our heart. When used responsibly, clothing can help us close that gap, give us a boost, or even transform our inner beauty in permanent ways.

Take, for example, the term "power suit." When a man or woman puts on a power suit, they feel invincible, in control, and ready to take on the world. My own power suit would include a brightly colored dress and a good pair of heels. The height from the heels and the color from the dress give me a literal and figurative boost, and I feel more confident, like I can accomplish anything. In the "right" outfit, I am more likely to give a quality presentation, land the job, and make better connections with those around me.

When you wear a power suit, you are not more successful because of the suit. It's not our outfit that lights up the room, or makes people like us or hire us. The suit in this case is actually changing you from the inside out. Wearing our clothing as armor helps us tap into our true confidence that comes from within, the confidence that is firmly rooted in the belief that we were made in God's image, and that the source of our beauty is not external but a result of our "inner self, the unfading beauty of a gentle and quiet spirit." It's not the suit but our confidence that affects our experience in positive ways.

Much like Iron Man's, our superpowers are temporary, and when we take the suit off, those powers have the potential to leave us. But sometimes changes to our external appearance wind up permanently changing our thoughts, our mind, and our relationships. In college, I transitioned from the temporary confidence that came from my clothing to true inner confidence pretty quickly. Wearing cute clothes was the crutch I needed to get past my social phobias. Once I put myself out there and tried, I realized that socializing wasn't scary, it was actually really fun. I moved past a dependence on my external appearance for my confidence and found a wellspring of true confidence that stemmed from my inner beauty that I operate with to this day.

We see this idea play out on makeover and weight-loss shows all the time. When someone is given a new hairstyle, clothes, and makeup, it often transforms them on the inside, opening their heart and mind to the manners in which they can change their lives in real, meaningful ways. After receiving new wrapping paper in the form of clothes and makeup, women feel confident enough to finally go after the career they always wanted, take the scary step to mending relationships, or engage in other forms of self-care.

Sally had one such transformative experience. She went from hating her body to embracing and loving it, all because she started experimenting with clothing. She writes:

> I used to utilize so much energy hating my body that I exhausted myself into depression. For years I tried to change my body with diets and exercise, believing that its shape and size were the root of the problem, but I just kept on hating it. When I began exploring fashion and style—dressing in fun, flattering, and form-fitting clothes—an unexplored universe opened up to me. For the first time, I respected my body. I realized that there was nothing wrong with my body. I saw my body as integral to my identity. I wanted to

show it off, and decorate it joyously, and hone my personal style so that I could understand it on new levels.[1]

When someone is feeling low and not loving her body, clothing sometimes has the power to change her mind, much like it did for Sally. Without even realizing it, women will use clothing to shame themselves, excessively covering things they don't like or want to hide. Or they keep wearing a too-small size, ashamed of going to a bigger size, which can compound a lack of confidence. When your clothes don't fit, it's easy to believe that your body is the issue and not the clothes. Hidden behind those clothes, the beautiful woman inside has a metaphorical and physical barrier to interacting with the world in a real and vulnerable way.

Imagine for a moment that you spent years cultivating the most exquisite gift that is "worth far more than rubies" (Proverbs 31:10, NIV). Now imagine that precious gift is wrapped in old newspaper and smeared with dog poo. We can all name amazing women with hearts of gold who aren't wearing the wrapping paper to match. Does their wrapping paper change the fact that they have hearts of gold? Absolutely not. Those of us lucky enough to know them know what gems they are, with or without the fancy wrapping paper on the outside. And yet we do long for the world to see the beauty that we see! We want the women with massive amounts of inner beauty to be so confident with their beauty that they want to celebrate with a big, shiny bow.

For example, one way women commonly shame themselves is by believing they need to lose weight. Clothing has the power to transform the image you see in the mirror because the right dress can trim pounds, work magic, and mold a body in ways you can't imagine. But it also has the power to transform the mind of the person wearing it. Seeing

---

1   Sally McGaw, "Mission Statement," *Already Pretty* (blog), November 30, 2010, http://www.alreadypretty.com/mission-statement.

yourself in the right dress can be a wonderful reminder of how beautiful you are. I personally believe that the most successful weight-loss journey begins with a mind that feels love and houses positive thoughts about one's own body. Weight loss that comes from a place of hate or shame never seems to work very well, at least it doesn't for me.

By dressing your body beautifully, in the state it's in right now, you are physically manifesting the idea that you accept your body, no matter what. When we shrink away and don't want anything to do with our wrapping paper, we are saying to ourselves and others, "I can't be beautiful, or I'm not worth beautiful wrapping paper until I do X, Y, or Z." But when we embrace our wrapping paper, we are living out our belief in our own inner beauty. We are dressing for the inside and celebrating the internal beauty that God sees.

Clothing, makeup, and hair can be powerful tools for change when used responsibly, in a positive way. But there is also a negative side. When our outer wrapper has the power to make us feel good, then it may also possess the power to make us feel very, very bad. Using a "power suit" to help your mood or confidence in certain situations is one thing, but relying on it too heavily or letting clothing and makeup dictate how you feel is entirely something else.

When Clothing Is Our Crutch

It's tough to believe I was ever shy, because these days I'm superoutgoing and like to work the room. But on this particular night, minutes before I was due to walk the runway for a charity I love, I was hunkered down, away from the crowd. As I observed the other local "celebrities" who were walking the runway interacting with one another, happy elated sounds and bursts of laughter drifted my way. No one else seemed nervous. But to me, this runway walk felt more like walking the plank. My hands were in a cold sweat, and I just wanted to get it over with.

The event was an annual fundraiser for one of my favorite fair-trade ethical fashion brands, and just being there was an honor—the other invitees were some of my favorite local news anchors, politicians, and athletes. I'm no stranger to stages and speaking engagements, and while I had little to no runway experience, I had no reason to think that it would be anything but fun. But I was wrong.

It took some time for me to fully dissect why I had a panic attack that night. I was embarrassed to realize that it stemmed from my being uncomfortable with my outer appearance, and touting it on the runway, in front of a crowd. Normally I'm in the driver's seat of my own clothing, hair, and makeup, but that night all control was relinquished to a team of stylists. It's not that I thought they didn't do a good job. I just felt unlike myself in heavy, sparkly makeup, dark lipstick, and an elaborate updo. (I prefer a more natural look, like minimal makeup and the hairstyle you will almost always find me rocking: "down.") I was already in unfamiliar territory because I was about to be judged by hundreds of people based solely on my outer appearance—I wasn't giving a speech or adding value with my personality or mind. And with my clothing, hair, and makeup feeling so alien to me that night, I completely clammed up.

My experience reminds me of an episode of *The Tyra Banks Show* I saw many years ago. The guest that day was a girl with an extreme phobia of being seen without makeup. Tyra challenged her to take off all her makeup and walk outside, and she had an actual meltdown, right there on TV. I'm sure it was partly for the entertainment factor and partly for ratings, but it also created a good opportunity for a self-check-in: Do I rely on makeup and clothing a little *too* much?

Ashley Marin, founder of Marin Makeup, says that until she discovered the true source of and confidence in her inner beauty that comes from Christ, her use of makeup did not come from a healthy place. "I really wore makeup to hide who I was. I had to look 'just right' to walk into a room, and I had to have a big smile on my face. I was never really able to be me."

My runway-show experience and Tyra's guest are two extreme examples of the negative powers that our clothing/hair/makeup potentially hold. For most of us, in most situations, not having the right wrapping paper will not result in an actual meltdown. It's more like mild indigestion—we may feel some discomfort from time to time. Like when we show up wearing red to an all-white event, or you're wearing jeans when everyone else is in cocktail attire. It's not fun, but, ideally, it doesn't ruin our night.

I've experienced this type of fashion fail too many times to count. I'll leave the house feeling great about my outfit, only to discover I've badly miscalculated and it doesn't fit the occasion. I once put on a head-to-toe neon outfit for a birthday party. I was feeling great and rocking those bright colors. But then I walked into the party and discovered that everyone else was wearing plaid, dark denim, and leather jackets. I was dressed for Miami, while everyone else was dressed for a hipster log cabin in Vermont. Another time, in my early twenties, I was tasked with bringing a TV personality to a station event for work, so I asked the host what the dress code was. They mentioned jeans, so I wore jeans and a collared shirt—only to discover that literally no one else was wearing jeans, and I was way too casual. They most likely meant jeans for the TV personality, since he worked in construction and that's what he wore on the TV show. Whoops!

On the occasions when our wrapping paper is not what we would like it to be, our external appearance may suddenly feel like a detriment, or like a hurdle to jump over, blocking people from being able to see or get to know our true beauty within. I think that discomfort is totally normal (nobody likes to be "that girl"), but when do our feelings about wearing no makeup, too much makeup, or not the right outfit cross into shallow territory?

My panic attack at the runway show was a wake-up call for me. While we certainly shouldn't shame ourselves for feeling uncomfortable, we also shouldn't let those situations affect our confidence in our true inner beauty, especially when our faith and definition of beauty stands on the solid rock of Jesus. We can and should rest knowing that our true confidence is not derived from our appearance at all, and that our beauty comes from within (as we discussed in chapter 4). In those uncomfortable situations, we know we are beautiful because we are made in God's image, and that nothing on our external bodies can ever take away from that. Our loved ones will not or should not love us any less because we are wearing jeans to a dressy party, and if our exterior is really that much of a barrier to a stranger, then it's probably not a huge loss that they are left as just that—a stranger. Much in the same way taking a moment to apply makeup or fix our hair before we leave the house gets our outer appearance ready, spending time in prayer and reflecting on the principles and true definition of beauty helps prepare our hearts before we walk out the door.

I was given an opportunity to test my newfound resolve on this subject six months later. I did a photo shoot for *Orange Appeal* magazine, and throughout the course of a day, they put me in eleven different outfits and changed my hair and makeup just as many times. Some of the clothing was exquisite (they had more than $100,000 worth of clothes on set!), and many of the makeup techniques were gorgeous. I thought about my panic attack on my way to the photo shoot that morning, and I resolved to walk in confident in the beauty that comes from my own heart and mind, and the peace that comes from knowing my true worth in Christ. Throughout the day, there were several moments when I did feel uncomfortable with what I was wearing (not all eleven outfits were "me"), or with the color of my lipstick (lipstick is my kryptonite—it's so far out of my usual lip-gloss comfort zone). But I did not experience even the slightest hint of nervousness or panic (just some of that mild discomfort I described earlier). It went off without a hitch and I enjoyed myself immensely. More than anything, it was fun!

Analyzing our reaction to events like these, both real and imagined, is a great way to do a self-check-in. But it's also just skimming the surface. While we can use our outer wrapping to help us connect to the true unadorned and irrefutable beauty that God sees in all of us, we can also find ourselves spending damaging amounts of time and money on our outer appearance, or doing it for all the wrong reasons.

When Clothing Is Our Vice

Clothing, hair, and makeup are exciting. There are more magazines and websites dedicated to these topics than one can count. Shopping is a popular pastime, used as a fun way to connect with our friends, reward ourselves for an accomplishment, or unwind and relax. For many of us, when we shop, endorphins are released into our brain, making us feel good. Fashion can be good, clean fun, in many ways. But when do we cross over the safe zone and into the "too much fun" zone?

The checkpoints for determining when we've had too much fun—when clothing has become our vice—are in many respects the same or similar to the ones we talked about in chapter 4. Our attempt to control our second layer of beauty—our body and skin—can manifest in ways that are similar to our attempt to control our third layer of beauty—our clothing, hair, and makeup.

One of the easiest ways to get ourselves in trouble is by spending too much time and money on makeup and clothes. Many of us, myself included, have had moments of overspending or buying something we later regret. For some people, though, it's a full-fledged addiction that has big life consequences, leaving their finances, health, and personal relationships in shambles. Take these two real-life examples from a 2009 Los Angeles Times article:

Anika Jackson, 34, identifies herself as a shopaholic. . . . Growing up in Kansas, she used to buy ball gowns for no reason and as a young raver, she owned "50 miniskirts with matching accessories." Today, Jackson is the mother of a 9-month-old daughter whose closet is filled with clothes that will keep her well-dressed until she's 3—"too cute to pass up." These days, Jackson's most effective way of avoiding spending is simply to stay out of stores, "because if I walk in somewhere, I will find something that I like." She cannot enter Anthropologie without spending "$800 to $1,000."

Marika Krissman Tsircou, 36, of Los Feliz, a friend of Jackson's and a fellow shopaholic, says that she receives so many packages from her online purchases, her UPS man knows her dogs by name. "Someone has to keep the economy going, right?" she jokes.[2]

As a result of my upbringing and personality, I've always been quite the opposite of a shopaholic. If anything, there have been times in my life when I wasn't spending enough time and money on clothing. My desire to work through the guilt I experience when I buy something, even when I really need it, is one thing that led me to start a fashion blog in the first place. Over the years I've realized that I'm prone to a much different and yet related vice—judging and evaluating shopping and vanity in excess, both in myself and in others.

Laura knows this struggle well. As she shared in an interview, her focus on not being vain became a vice itself.

---

2 Steffie Nelson, "Real-Life Shopaholics in a World of Hurt," *Los Angeles Times*, February 8, 2009, http://articles.latimes.com/2009/feb/08/image/ig-shopaholics8/2.

On one hand, I will compare myself to the legalistic types who view any sort of attention you spend on your appearance to be of the flesh. My internal dialogue says: *She must truly be filled with the Holy Spirit on a level far greater than I am,* or, *Appearance must not matter that much to her. Am I sinning because I do care about appearance?*

On the other hand, I will compare myself to the "selfie" women—the ones who are always gorgeous and know it, and often post countless filtered pics of their face, outfits of the day, and exercise regimens. With them, I find myself totally judging them for being more concerned with outward appearance than the condition of their hearts.

While spending too much time or money on fashion—or judging others who do so—are common vices to avoid, they aren't the only ones we should be mindful of. Indulging in fashion for the wrong reasons—to win the approval of those around us, or to fill a void within ourselves—are also cause for concern. Sometimes we may focus on our outer appearance to mask, disguise, or distract from an inner problem of the heart.

Avis is an author and a journalist, and a recovering shopping addict. She was focused on her outer appearance as a way to fill a void left by her mother's passing and depression brought on by low self-esteem. She says:

When I've analyzed my own shopping addiction I realized that the event that precipitated excessive shopping was my mother's death. I couldn't cope with that tragedy and shopping came to the rescue. It was an activity in which I could hide. Part of my hiding meant hiding behind a mask of perfection. Therefore, clothing, accessories, and cosmetics became the tools of creating that perfect me.³ When we look to fill a void in our hearts and lives with shopping (or any other worldly pursuit), we will never be fully satisfied or happy—no matter how many clothes we own. Any happiness we derive from our vice is bound to last a short time, maybe even a few days, but it always fades away. In the movie *Confessions of a Shopaholic*, main character Rebecca Bloomwood explains how quickly shopping makes her feel empty again, saying, "Because when I shop the world gets better. The world is better. And then it's not anymore. And I need to do it again."⁴

In the documentary *The True Cost*, Tim Kasser, PhD, a psychology professor at Knox College, explains:

> What we now know, [after] twenty years and hundreds of studies, is that the more people focus on these materialistic values, the more that money and image, and its status and possessions are important to them, the less happy they are, and the more depressed and anxious they are. These types of psychological problems, they tend to increase when increasing materialistic values. [Which] is in total disagreement with the thousands of messages we receive daily from ads suggesting that materialism and the pursuit of possessions and owning things is what will make us happy.

Just as we can look to God to define our inner beauty, we can turn to Him to satisfy our thirst and complete our emptiness. Away from the

---

3   "Avis Cardella: Confessions of a Real-Life Shopaholic," interview by Trisha Ping, *BookPage*, May 2010, https://bookpage.com/interviews /8596-avis-cardella.

4   "*Confessions of a Shopaholic* Script – Dialogue Transcript," Script-O -Rama.com, accessed June 11, 2017, http://www.script-o-rama.com /movie_scripts/a1/confessions-of-a-shopaholic-script.html.

noise of advertising, peer pressure, or our own insecurities, we find what we are looking for in His presence. "You, God, are my God, earnestly I seek you; I thirst for you, my whole being longs for you, in a dry and parched land where there is no water" (Psalm 63:1, NIV).

Oftentimes the void we are trying to fill is wrapped up in the opinions of others. When that's the case, our focus on fashion doesn't arise from a healthy sense of inner beauty or for our own creative expression and pleasure. Rather, it becomes way too much about the reaction of others. If we post an outfit on Instagram, for example, and we measure its success solely by how many "likes" it gets, we are missing the point entirely. The same is true when we use our clothing and makeup to not really tell the whole truth, when we use them as a mask to cover what we perceive as outer beauty deficiencies, or to hide a deficiency or source of insecurity in our hearts.

Imagine that you have packed a gift box full of rocks, with little to no value, but you've spent hours wrapping it in the most expensive, flashy wrapping paper. The paper may make you more excited about presenting your gift to the world, and it may also attract a lot of attention, but when the recipient opens the gift, what will happen? When they dig deeper into your heart, what will they find?

At the very worst, we can fall victim to wanting or expecting our wrapping to be the gift itself. When our outer wrapper is hiding a deficiency in spirit, or a matter of the heart, then the truth will come out eventually. As we learned in chapter 4, beauty is fleeting; it does not last. Like wrapping paper it is eventually discarded into the trash, leaving us only with the gift inside. Our outer wrapper in the world's eyes is only good until the next fashion trend comes out the next day. Only our inner, true beauty in Christ withstands the test of time and will be the way in which God—our one and only true judge—will measure our worth.

Clothing is a vice when we have an emotional breakdown without it, or can't carry on because we feel so uncomfortable with what we are wearing. Clothing is a vice when we don't just desire it, we require it, or when we find that we can't or don't feel beautiful without it. Clothing is a vice when we spend all the money we have to fill a void, only to find ourselves empty again and seeking more. Clothing is a vice when we try to define our own beauty with clothing, hair, and makeup, rather than trusting in our own internal beauty from and in Christ.

A Healthy Third Layer: Our Relationship with Clothes

The cry of my heart is this: to be able to truthfully go to my closet with these words on my heart and on my lips: These things in my closet have the power to boost my confidence, but they are not the source of my confidence. These things in my closet have the ability to tell the world things about my personality, but they are not the source of my personality. These things in my closet have the ability to make me feel beautiful, but they are not the source of my beauty.

Recognizing the power that clothes hold over us is an important first step to a healthy relationship with our third layer. Because while clothing, hair, and makeup can make us feel great, they can also make us feel not so great. Having an inner foundation of strength in Christ makes us invincible to a darker side of clothing, to the risk of allowing clothing to control us. Clothing may reflect our inner thoughts, it may communicate them to the world, but, in the end, you are wearing the clothes, the clothes are not wearing you.

To find where you stand, you may ask yourself, *What is my motivation behind my outward adornment? Am I using clothing and makeup as false confidence, to fill a hole in my self-esteem or feel better about myself, or as a way to impress someone? Or is my outward adornment part of my creativity and self-expression that satisfies my soul and honors God?* Sometimes we may find that it's easier to build our confidence around external decorum, but it's certainly not better. Like most things that are of the world, it's the house that's build on sand. Depending on our outer appearance for confidence all the time is like a diet of all junk food—it's a quick fix and it's cheap, but it's not healthy.

For me, the true magic of clothing happens when you forget what you are wearing at all. Spending a little bit of time on our outer appearance upfront means it won't be a distraction throughout your day—you won't have to worry about being too dressed up or not dressy enough, too hot or too cold. It's never my goal to be too confident in what I'm wearing (showing off). I just want to clear my mind of my outer appearance, so I can focus on the precious memories I'm making.

Consider this humbling thought from lead pastor Justin Johnson of One Church Park District in Winter Park, Florida:

> Jesus hung naked and exposed on the cross, so that you never have to fear being exposed. Through the gospel, clothes are no longer a façade to hide behind, but a mirror to reflect the glory and beauty within.

When we find peace with the wrapping paper that encircles our precious hearts and bodies, we can truly know, understand, and pursue the true definition of beauty, and practice it in our daily lives with ourselves and others. When we come from that place, our outward adornment is not and does not become sin, or vanity, or shallowness. It is our expression of worship, our expression of creativity, and an expression of our deepest joy.

Chapter 6

What Is Modesty?

The modesty discussion often dominates the world of Christian fashion more than any other topic. By definition, a "Christian fashion blogger" or "Christian Fashion Week" generally means a heavy focus on modesty. For me, combining the two worlds of fashion and faith means so much more—being a good steward of the environment and our money, giving thought to fair wages, and avoiding the temptation of vanity or greed, to name a few (all topics we'll discuss at length in upcoming chapters). But modesty is often the biggest fashion banner you will find flying in Christian culture, due in part to this verse from 1 Timothy 2:9–10:

> I also want the women to dress modestly, with decency and propriety, adorning themselves, not with elaborate hairstyles or gold or pearls or expensive clothes, but with good deeds, appropriate for women who profess to worship God. (NIV)

We had a very strict dress code at the Christian high school I attended. We were not allowed to wear shorts of any length, tank tops of any kind, and sweatshirts (which killed me; I loved hoodies), and our shirts had to be tucked in at all times. I got detention all the time for not meeting the dress code. As a teenager, I never quite made a conscious connection between my high school dress code and modesty. In many ways I thought the school was just trying to control us—the hoodie thing, for example, was an effort to get us to look more presentable or dressed up. I didn't think about modesty much: I just always wanted to wear "whatever I want." Even today, at times, the notion of modesty seriously cramps my style. If you tell me there's a fashion rule of any kind, like don't wear navy and black together, or no white jeans after Labor Day, then I immediately want to break it: I think it's just in my DNA!

But modesty, I will admit, is not always something to be flippant about. It's an incredibly complex issue that involves so many things: important cultural norms, sex and attraction, and self-esteem. But most importantly, it's about honoring God with our bodies. A direct command to dress "modesty, with decency and propriety" is right there in the Bible. My insistence on wearing "whatever I want" is certainly never intended to disobey this direct order. But the issue for me becomes this: If we are to obey this command, then how do we define the rules? Because the verse and the Bible in general certainly leave a whole lot open to interpretation. What exactly *is* modesty?

How much and what parts of her body can a woman show? Does it depend on where she is, both geographically and socially? Is modesty solely a women's issue, and if not, what role do men have on the topic of modesty? The answer to all these questions, I believe, is a resounding, and frustrating, "It all depends."

Modesty Issue #1: Geography and Culture

The farther we traveled into the remote villages of India, the more uncomfortable I became. Dressed in a loose denim dress worn over white jeans, with a big scarf around my neck, I was certainly in modest attire by American standards. And my outfit was similar in shape to those of the Indian women around me—they often wear long tunics over leggings or pants. But I still couldn't shake the feeling that I was offending someone, if the stares were any indication. I wore the scarf around my neck for extra bust coverage, but I wound up using it in another way. Once inside the village, I pulled it over my head to conceal my hair and shield my face, taking modesty a step further. I certainly wasn't looking to raise eyebrows with what I was wearing, and I hoped that the scarf over my head would help.

Whenever I travel to another country for the first time, I like to do some research or ask a trip leader about the cultural context of where we are going. That's because the rules for modesty are not standardized, by any means. In some parts of Africa, women walk around topless to make breastfeeding easier, but skinny jeans are out, because women's butts and thighs are more sexualized in those cultures. In India, women sometimes wear crop tops under their saris, and you may see stomachs showing, but ankles and legs are to be kept private and covered. In America, women show their legs with shorts, but breasts are sexualized and should be covered, to the point of policing mothers who are breastfeeding in public. There is certainly not one global standard for modesty by any stretch of the imagination.

When I travel, I usually err on the side of caution. As a representative of my own (American) culture, I would never want to offend someone else's culture. It's a sign of respect to adhere to the modesty standards in the country you are traveling in, even if you can't fathom why ankles are so sexy and need to be covered up.

Since there isn't one overarching standard of modesty across the world, though, the Biblical command for modesty can feel tricky to adhere to. First and foremost, what's considered "modest" depends on your geography. With some research, we can define the overall standards of modesty in any one country, but we still have the idiosyncrasies of the cultures within that country to dissect. I found differing standards among different parts of India. And here in America we often find vastly different dress codes between regions, states, and even right down to the molecular level of what's okay and what's not okay to wear at specific churches and places of employment.

In the list of Fashion Commandments on my blog, I say that, in essence, you should wear whatever you want and not worry about what anyone thinks—with two noted exceptions, which are modesty at church and at work. In these two places, you generally care greatly about your relationship with those around you, and showing respect is important. I might wear whatever I want to the grocery store, because I don't have a relationship with the people in the store. They are not my coworkers, my boss, my church congregation, or my pastor, and since their opinions don't count on that same level, I'm free from most (but not all) modesty standards and dress code requirements.

Certainly churches and office buildings aren't the only exceptions to the "wear what you want" rule, though. There are bound to be places specific to your own life, like your in-laws' house, or an event at a conservative company, where you may choose to be extra careful about what you wear. And in some cases, just visiting a church means showing respect with modesty in a very particular way. In Italy, skimpy dresses are okay out on the streets, but when you enter a church they ask you to tie a scarf around your shoulders to cover up (they actually provide scarves as you walk through the door, in case you don't have your own). I may not know anyone in that church or care what they think as individuals, but I will absolutely show respect for the church as an institution in whatever way local custom requires, so please hand me that scarf.

Because we are in "God's house," I think the appropriateness of our dress comes under extra scrutiny in our churches. But just as different countries and regions have different taboos and norms when it comes to what we can wear, so do different congregations. Jeans and flip-flops are the norm in the church we now attend here in Florida, but in another church I occasionally attended up north, the norm was full suits and Sunday best. Some churches will frown upon bright colors or flashy fashion statements, whereas others encourage full brim hats with big bows. I've lived in and attended churches in three parts of the country—the Midwest (Kansas), the Northeast (Boston) and the South (Orlando)—and the cultural differences I've seen within our own nation are astounding, and something I think people often take for granted.

I once posted an outfit I was planning to wear to church that included hot pink heels, and it was called a "lady of the night" look (and worse) by commenters. Putting aside the question of whether that kind of language is ever within the realm of helpful feedback, I think people sometimes forget that what's not acceptable at the church they attend might be just fine in other parts of the country, or even the church next door to theirs. We enjoy a lot of freedom in America—within the same country we have the Duggars and the Playboy Bunnies—and with that freedom comes a lot of variance in dress code. It trickles down to the most minute differences, depending on your location, industry, and plain ol' personal taste.

I have always hesitated to write about modesty on my blog, because the rules are not standardized and it's tough to generalize. What skin is okay to show in one country is different in the next. What's okay to wear in one church isn't okay in the other. What's okay in one office building isn't okay in another one. And modesty is only one part of the puzzle. Covering up is one issue, but we would also be remiss not to consider how casual or dressy we should be, and whether things like bright colors are frowned upon. (That is, if we are looking to blend in. We may not, after all, be the "tan and navy" type from chapter 2.) And, while we've talked a lot about the rules that govern heels and hats, bellies and breasts, what about the rules for modesty as they apply to men?

Modesty Issue #2: The Men Around Us

Identifying what's modest from one culture to the next is mostly surface talk. Because the underlying question is: Why are those parts of a
woman's body considered "immodest" in the first place? When we dig
deeper, we find that what's really at the core of modesty are bombshell
topics like sex, attraction, and gender roles. Have you ever wondered,
why aren't men asked to cover up too? In India, women are often covered from head to toe, but men freely drop their pants and urinate on
the side of the road. Is modesty a women's issue, about women's bodies?
Or is it a men's issue, about how they react to women's bodies?

From a Christian standpoint, the issue of modesty and the desire to
cover women up comes largely from Matthew 5:28. Matthew presents
the idea that when women dress immodestly, we are tempting men to
sin in their hearts, and tempting them to sin with their bodies (if they
choose to act on those thoughts). "But I tell you that anyone who looks
at a woman lustfully has already committed adultery with her in his
heart" (Matthew 5:28, NIV).

Part of me insists that we can't control how other people think
or behave. When I make a style decision, like wearing pink and red
together, and it really bothers someone reading my blog ("It hurts my
eyes!" they might say), I want to tell them to just look away! Adopting
that same approach here, it sometimes feels unfair that women have to
cover up because men are struggling with sin. If a woman wearing yoga
pants or breastfeeding in public gives a man impure thoughts, why does
the onus fall on the woman? Why isn't the focus, instead, on teaching
men to control those thoughts? Is modesty really a women's issue after
all, or is this really more about men?

While I believe we shouldn't always place the reactions of men
entirely upon women's shoulders, I can also empathize with some of the
issues that men struggle with. I've had heart-to-heart conversations with
Christian men who, despite their faith, struggle with porn addiction,

lust, or sex addictions. Knowing what they go through and how dedicated they are to recovery, I'm inclined to want to help them out in any way I can. Immodesty is a visual sin—once they see it, it's often too late. You wouldn't tempt a recovering alcoholic by offering them a drink. And, in this situation, what does covering up really hurt?

A friend telling me that seeing a woman breastfeeding in church tortures his soul makes me say, "Why not choose modesty for our fellow brothers in Christ?" It also makes me question how men ended up like this in the first place. How much should we expect men to just get ahold of themselves, and how much of the blame should rest with our culture's obsession with sexualizing women?

During one of my trips abroad, a man on the street grabbed my butt. I really wouldn't have thought much of it, because we were in a super-crowded market and it felt like an accident. But then the man came around and got in my face, making sure I knew it was him. My first thought was, Am I not dressed modestly enough? Am I offending him? I immediately blamed myself, which I have to say is so frustrating. I was dressed very modestly, in baggy pants and a long baggy shirt, with not an ounce of skin or my shape showing. But as women we often blame ourselves and feel like we did something wrong. Are the same cultures that are teaching men it's okay to grab women also teaching women that it's our fault for not covering up enough? And are these cultures teaching us that we are somehow capable of controlling what men think about us by choosing to wear one outfit over another? How much should I be expected to change about myself before I can expect men to behave?

In the Bible, Jesus spends a lot of time with tax collectors and prostitutes. When I picture this group, I can't imagine that they weren't often dressed provocatively. Was Jesus tempted? Wasn't He afraid the disciples would fall into sin? I love the way Jonathan Trotter puts it in *Relevant* magazine:[1]

> I believe Jesus wasn't afraid because He saw their humanity. And He knew that their humanity desperately needed His divinity. To love people is to be with people. And people don't always follow "the rules" or dress "appropriately." If we can't figure out how to deal with that, we're going to have a heck of a hard time sharing Jesus with folks who don't know Him and act like it. And that just might be the saddest thing of all.

Now let's go even deeper and dive down into the next layer. Because our bodies have a lot more dimensions than just what men think about them—we are far more complex than that, ladies! Our relationship with our own bodies is important and compounds the issue further. Sometimes modesty isn't about sex or men at all.

Modesty Issue #3: Our Relationship with Our Own Bodies

Wearing nothing but a bikini and high heels, my friend Monica stepped onto the stage amid screams and cheering. Her spray tan was glowing, her legs were waxed, her makeup was professionally applied, and she was ready to present her body to the world. Her reason for doing so, though, might surprise you.

After giving birth to her third child, Monica hated how she looked. She struggled with feeling pretty around her husband and felt unhappy and unhealthy. So she started working out regularly and eating healthy,

---

[1]   Jonathan Trotter, "The Lies Modesty Culture Teaches Men," *Relevant*, September 7, 2016, http://www.relevantmagazine.com/god/worldview /lies-modesty-culture-teaches-men.

and she lost seventy-five pounds in eighteen months. After three babies, her body may not have been "perfect," but to celebrate her success and challenge herself further, she entered into a fitness model competition, complete with a bikini round that would require (gulp) wearing next to nothing on stage.

Walking a runway in a bikini and high heels is not the shining ideal of modesty, no matter the culture. But Monica's story illustrates that sometimes, sex appeal and how men feel about our bodies has absolutely nothing to do with the situation at hand. Perhaps there was a man in the audience who was aroused by Monica's appearance. We can't know for sure. But it was the furthest thing from Monica's mind that day, and the bikini competition for her was in fact strengthening her relationship with the most important people in her world: her husband and her children. By losing the weight and getting healthy, Monica had more energy to play with her kids and more confidence around her husband, and the runway was a declaration and a celebration of that.

Sometimes as women, and especially as women of faith, we have a hard time believing that immodesty is ever innocent. We all know someone who has used low-cut shirts or a tight dress for the expressed goal of finding a man or to get "that kind" of attention. When my friend Katie was in high school, she purposely wore high heels and a short skirt to turn heads. (It worked, and it made her more popular, but it was the wrong kind of attention, and it's a big part of her testimony today.) But while it's easy to always associate skimpy clothes, heels, or a bikini with less-than-wholesome motives, that's not always the case.

I had a moment recently when I judged someone's intentions too quickly. I read a headline about a woman who'd been kicked out of a Missouri water park for dressing immodestly, and I assumed her intentions were not all positive. It turns out that she was on a weight-loss journey much like Monica's. She shared in the article that she used to be overweight and had been so ashamed of her body before that she wouldn't even show the skin on her arms and legs, let alone the parts exposed when you wear a bikini. Now that she's lost a hundred pounds and is in great shape, she's proud of her physique. She was wearing a bikini just like everyone else's, with full-coverage bottoms, but her confidence was not sitting well with the people around her. (Maybe she looked a little *too* good?) Because she's in her forties and has full hips and a large bust, the article theorized that she'd been subjected to age and body-type discrimination. No matter the cause for her removal, I was happily put in my place for judging too quickly. Good for her for feeling comfortable in her own skin!

I can say from experience that donning a tight dress doesn't always mean you're interested in turning heads or turning anyone on. In my midtwenties I wore a short, tight dress for my birthday one year, and it had everything to do with a very personal journey toward confidence, and absolutely nothing to do with attracting male attention. Around the same time, I arranged to have a girlfriend who was just starting her photography career take some outfit photos of me that I would describe as "sexy" (if I could keep a straight face and call myself that). I'm sure people could have assumed I was just trying to attract attention. But I was, like Monica, going through a transformation and a celebration of my body that was completely my own.

While my "immodest" birthday dress was about expressing something very personal, some women dress a certain way—or not—to rebel against body shaming or our society's very particular beauty standards. A great example of this is Paulette Leaphart, a breast cancer survivor who recently walked a thousand miles from Mississippi to Washington, DC, completely topless.[2] Her breasts were removed in a double mastectomy in 2014, and for health reasons she wasn't a candidate for breast implants. Paulette's journey, was not about attracting male attention.

---

2   Patrick Clarke, "Breast Cancer Survivor Will Walk 1,000 Miles to Congress," ABC News, April 29, 2016, http://abcnews.go.com/Lifestyle /breast-cancer-survivor-walk-1000-miles-congress/story?id=38538370.

Her goal was to raise awareness about breast cancer and show other survivors there is no reason to be ashamed of their scars.

I mentioned Taryn Brumfitt, founder of the Body Image Movement, in chapter 4. She hated the way her body looked after having kids, telling herself in the mirror, "You're fat. You are ugly. You are disgusting."[3] She hated the way her body looked so much that she booked plastic surgery for her breasts and tummy. In a fit of inspiration, though, Taryn canceled her procedures and posted a nude photo of herself online. The image went viral, and now she has written a book and produced a documentary, both called *Embrace*, about loving our bodies just the way that they are. *Embrace* ads have been banned from Facebook and the movie has been blocked from some theaters because of the nudity, which is unfortunate because the nudity in the film has little to do with being provocative and everything to do with making a statement about body shaming.

Sometimes a woman's immodesty isn't about making any type of statement. Rather, it's about utility. During the Olympics in Rio last summer the team uniforms of some of the female beach-volleyball players caused quite a stir. It never would've occurred to me that Olympic athletes were being immodest in a sexual way, but a social media post from a parody account went viral in which the guy was—how do I put this—sexualizing them in a pretty gross manner.[4]

It makes sense that divers and swimmers wear swimsuits, so why not beach volleyball players? The tight material keeps sand out of places it shouldn't go, and the relatively small amount of cloth keeps them cool in the hot sun and doesn't weigh them down. The reality that men are

---

3   Taryn Brumfitt, *Body Image Movement* (blog), accessed June 11, 2017, https://bodyimagemovement.com.
4   Will Ferrell, Twitter post, January 30, 2013, 12:33 p.m., https://twitter.com/will_ferreii/status/296717770756853761?lang=en.

going to look doesn't go away, but that also has nothing to do with why the women are wearing these outfits.

In some cases, a person who dresses immodestly may not even be aware of it. I hope you won't mind me sharing a confession with you all here in this book (You guys can keep a secret, right?), but I struggle greatly in this area. In my logical mind, I know that men may lust for a woman when they see her walking around with a low-cut top or short shorts. But my emotional heart tells me that it's not possible for *my* breasts or *my* body to turn men on. Don't get me wrong, I love my body to pieces, I just don't think of it as something to lust over. I'm so out of the loop I quite frankly forget that it's possible to be immodest with my body sometimes! (I'm working on it.)

This mental block results from a string of experiences in my past. In college I was told by someone I cared for that I would "be the perfect package if only I had breasts and a butt." I believed and internalized that his comment was true and that he was speaking for all men, and carried it with me for years. (Especially since his comment mirrored how I already felt about my body—I'm certainly flat allover, I'll give him that!) In my early twenties I got married after years of dedicating myself to celibacy. But, for complicated and private reasons that I won't disclose out of respect for my ex, the sexual experiences I'd been waiting for never came to fruition. It felt to me as if this was the tangible proof that all those beliefs and messages I'd received about not being sexy or sexually desirable were completely true.

What I hope all these stories illustrate is that it's not always about men. We don't always consciously think "this will or won't turn men on" when we put on shorts or a tank top. To me, the issue of "are men looking?" feels like it was answered years ago (with a resounding "no"), and I'm still trying to reverse those thought processes and beliefs that run so deep. You truly never know what baggage someone is carrying, and I'm sure I'm not the only one with this particular type of luggage in tow.

Certainly, we can all agree that sometimes a woman is in a swimsuit because it's hot and a swimsuit is the most practical thing to wear. Sometimes a woman is wearing a swimsuit because she underwent a huge body transformation and she's celebrating her success. Sometimes a woman goes nude to make a statement about body shaming. Sometimes a woman or girl is wearing short shorts and is completely oblivious to modesty concerns, or is naive to the fact that men are looking. We're going through our own journey with our bodies as women, and sometimes it's got little to do with anyone or anything else.

Policing Modesty

A wedding dress is probably the last thing you would imagine starting a controversy about modesty, but mine did. I was married for the second time to my wonderful husband, Joshua, in March 2015. A few months after our nuptials, I posted a picture of our wedding day on my blog's Facebook page. There were hundreds of comments wishing us congratulations, but there was also this comment:

> You are a beautiful woman. This dress just makes me sad though. You look like a lingerie model, not a bride. It's much more classy to be modest. Your children will see this, your grandmother will see this! I'm not saying you need to wear sleeves and a turtleneck, but are you really comfortable showing off all of your goods like that? I would feel naked, only covering my chest with some see through lace.

Reading something like this about your wedding day is jarring. We were surrounded by 120 of our closest friends and family; we were married by our pastor and his wife, with his father (also a pastor) and their extended family present. And someday, yes, our children might see the photos. In other words, of course I didn't want to be immodest!

The modesty question came up during wedding-dress shopping, but not in the way that commenter would expect. My very conservative Christian mother-in-law, who I love dearly, was shopping with me. When I tried on the dress, it was the runway sample and was cut so low in the front I had to hold it shut. I assured her that we would raise the neckline a good six inches (and we did, to the height of a normal V-neck), but she wasn't worried about it at all. She shared privately with me that while it was my own decision, she preferred the dress (that I ultimately picked) because it had straps, which in her eyes made it more modest than the strapless dresses I'd tried on. (A point of view that certainly not everyone shares, but a great example of how the definition of modesty can differ so greatly from one person to the next.)

Here's how I responded to the commenter on Facebook:

> You are also a beautiful woman! Is it possible you are projecting your own body and experiences? Because this sounds so different from what I felt. I chose this dress because I felt so much more laid back than anything with cups or an underwire (those dresses felt so overtly sexual on me!! so not my personality! I am the ultimate tomboy). I don't have any "goods" showing—there's no cleavage, I'm wearing a bra. I respect that you might feel naked, but I also ask that you respect that I didn't have the experience you are describing at all. I did choose modest, that word just sounds like it means something very different to me. <3

I think we tread on shaky ground when we try to police someone else's modesty. In the case of my wedding dress, we were talking about a wedding day—a sacred, holy day that's forever etched into time and can't be changed—so there's nothing really productive that can come from that conversation. What was her intended outcome? That I would go back in time and make a different decision? And why is the focus on what I'm wearing at all?

When we start debating whether shorts should be two inches longer, or a wedding dress neckline should be two inches higher or made out of a different material, we are arguing semantics in so many ways. People can be competitive about who follows the rules the most or the best, but when it comes to modesty, burkas are the gold standard, the highest level of modesty you can achieve. Why, then, argue over the length of shorts when all shorts are really technically immodest? And I have no idea what this commenter chose (or may choose) to wear on her wedding day, but unless she was only showing her eyeballs then she was also immodest—at least, by someone else's definition of the word. I hope that no one judged her that way, because how she chooses to define that word is something she should absolutely determine for herself.

Certainly modesty is an important topic to discuss with teenagers. I had my own teenage self in mind when I wrote this chapter—the things I wish I'd known and understood, like the way women's bodies are objectified, the struggle of some of our Christian brothers, the concept of body shaming, and what constitutes modesty in different cultures. All of these ideas are an important part of the conversation, but a deep look at each topic is far preferable to a blanket statement such as "cover up as much as possible" or "don't turn men on with your body," which leaves much to be desired.

A woman named Samantha shares her experience with that "cover it all" kind of modesty messaging as a teenager:

> I went to a youth group that was very keen on mod-
> esty. I remember getting kicked out of a youth car
> wash because my shirt covering my bathing suit wasn't

115

dark enough. I remember thinking, *Why does it matter,*
I'm wearing a shirt OVER my already modest one piece.
It was embarrassing and confusing to say the least.
Modesty is important. I don't need teen boys looking
at my booty in short shorts in high school. However,
if there is too much emphasis on modesty, especially
for girls, it can turn into self-conscious thoughts that
don't need to be there. While I truly believe modesty
is important, especially with young teen girls around
boys, I think there needs to be a healthy balance.

When it comes to policing modesty, there are times when a heads-
up, shared in a loving way with teenagers who really may not be aware
that guys are staring, is incredibly helpful. But it's also important not
to send the underlying message that all the blame and responsibility
should be put on the female. Or the message that "you are my competition and are attracting male attention, and I need you to cover up."
Or, "Your body has scars or cellulite or is just too much in general, and
is not adhering to society's standards of beauty." Modesty is already a
dynamic issue, with underlying misogynistic tensions fueled by men's
sexualizing women's bodies, and when we shame and victimize each
other as women, I think we are making the issue worse in so many ways.

We twist modesty into a knot when we start to define it the same
way the world (incorrectly) defines beauty. Is modesty really defined by
the reaction we get from those around us—that is, do we measure it
according to what other people think? (How men react, how women
judge us?) Some may believe beauty is defined by the world, how others may rank us, and adhering to society's standards means we have
achieved beauty. But being beautiful is defined by what's within (see
chapter 4), and the same goes for modesty. It's defined by the heart and
the intent of the person, not by the opinion of someone else viewing
that person from the outside. Isn't the heart behind that V-neck then,

and not the V-neck itself, what truly matters? "The Lord does not look at the things people look at. People look at the outward appearance, but the Lord looks at the heart" (1 Samuel 16:7, NIV).

I like my friend Sharon's take on the subject. On her blog, she uses the metaphor of your body as a Tiffany & Co. box to illustrate the importance of modest clothing:

> Each one of our bodies is as beautiful and precious as a perfect Tiffany diamond (and, yes, they come in all shapes, sizes, and colors). Our bodies are so precious and powerful that we have been given the gift of fabulous packaging. And that's why I personally believe that fashion has the potential for great holiness.[5]

When we consider the topic of modesty, I think we only need to ask, are we honoring God with our clothing decisions? Is modesty radiating from the inside out? Along the way you may encounter someone who questions you, like the reader who criticized my wedding dress or the person who sent Samantha home from the car wash. But let all that completely fade away for a moment. The noise of what men may think, what other women may think, what coworkers may think—let all of that completely wash away, and just focus on Him and His heart for your life. Ask God to show you what He desires from you when it comes to modesty. Because ultimately, it's not up to anyone else to define for us. What matters most is when we can confidently know in our hearts that our "inner modesty," is on point and honors God.

---

5   Sharon Langert, "Is Modesty a Form of Body Shaming?," Fashion-isha (blog), August 9, 2016, http://www.fashion-isha.com/2016/08/is -modesty-form-of-body-shaming.html.

Chapter 7

Is Fashion Selfish?

Four flights, a ferry ride, and eight hours in a truck over bumpy unpaved roads, and I was back at home in Orlando. My apartment felt strangely empty, like a vacant building with way too much space for one person. I had just spent two weeks in Sierra Leone with a team putting on a summer camp at a home for orphaned children. Reverse culture shock—the psychological, emotional, and cultural aspects of returning home after being submersed in another culture—often impacts those who have lived overseas for an extended period of time. But our trip to Sierra Leone was so intense, and so moving, that I was experiencing these symptoms after only two weeks.

The best way to describe it is that you can suddenly see "the Matrix." The normal things that I grew up with, that were once so common-place I barely even noticed their existence, now felt unnecessary and created an unfamiliar tug at my heart. Running water, electricity, grocery stores, air-conditioning, shopping malls—did we really need these things? What if it's all here just to distract us from our true meaning and purpose in life?

The basis of the Christian faith, and the mantra for many spiritual people no matter their religion, is to put others before yourself. I personally don't believe that I'm here on earth to pursue my own happiness or to "find happiness" but to be a blessing and a help to those around me. Even in marrying my husband, Joshua, I didn't just ponder whether doing so would bring value to my life, but also whether it would bring value to his. I reflected long and hard on whether I felt up to the task and whether I could bless him and his life's journey enough for our union to make sense. (A point of view earned from many years spent developing my emotional maturity; I can't say I've always approached relationships this way.)

It's the "golden rule" of Christianity—there is no greater command-ment than loving God and loving our neighbors before ourselves:

> Jesus answered him, "The first of all the command-ments is . . . you shall love the Lord your God with all your heart, with all your soul, with all your mind and with all your strength." . . . And the second . . . is this: "You shall love your neighbor as yourself." There is no commandment greater than these. (Mark 12:29–31, NKJV)

Around the holidays, Joshua and I like to make a list of twenty or so things we can do to honor this verse and put our neighbors, our com-munity, and even strangers before ourselves. The holidays are a good fit for this exercise for many reasons, but one major motivation is the amount of time I spend Christmas shopping. I really desire to balance what sometimes feels like a frivolous, self-centered activity with impor-tant activities that focus on the bigger picture. It's not all about having a Martha Stewart Christmas, but about those who have had a hard year and could really use an act of kindness or need food and supplies. It's following the example set forth in Matthew 25:35–40.

> "For I was hungry and you gave me something to eat, I was thirsty and you gave me something to drink, I was

a stranger and you invited me in, I needed clothes and you clothed me, I was sick and you looked after me, I was in prison and you came to visit me."

Then the righteous will answer him, "Lord, when did we see you hungry and feed you, or thirsty and give you something to drink? When did we see you a stranger and invite you in, or needing clothes and clothe you? When did we see you sick or in prison and go to visit you?"

The King will reply, "Truly I tell you, whatever you did for one of the least of these brothers and sisters of mine, you did for me." (NIV)

The problem with this "one in, one out" strategy—I spend one hour at the mall shopping, so I need to dedicate one hour to helping our neighbors in need—is that it leaves me feeling like my time is limited and cut into pieces like a pie. It also leads me to wonder why am I not giving the whole pie away, instead of using any of the pieces on "selfish" activities?

What I want to explore in this chapter is this: How much, really, should we give? Like, absolutely all of the possessions and money that we have? Or just some of it, while we keep some for ourselves to use on nice clothes, fancy dinners, and spa days? Are we really commanded to sell everything we own and give everything to the poor, like it says in Matthew 19:21? "Jesus said, 'If you want to be perfect, go, sell your possessions and give to the poor, and you will have treasure in heaven. Then come, follow me'" (NIV).

I will share some different perspectives in this chapter, including my own experiences. Ultimately it doesn't matter where I or anyone else draw this line, though. What matters is where you draw that line for yourself. We are commanded to give, and we should. But if we always give, a hundred percent of the time, then buying clothes for ourselves is basically off the table. Fashion for fun, or any of the arts—literature, music, film—are a moot point and should, if we get totally radical, be wiped from the face of the earth.

Throughout this book, we've discussed some compelling reasons why fashion should stay a part of this world. We looked at the importance of art in the struggle between good and evil, and at God's approval and appreciation of beauty (chapter 1); the soulful nature of our innate passion for art as humans (chapter 2); the necessity of clothes (chapter 3); and the important relationship that clothing has with our inner beauty (chapters 4–5). As the list goes on, it seems like Matthew 19:21 may not be our only guidepost to consider when answering the questions: Is fashion selfish? So where do we draw that line for ourselves? Let's consider some perspectives.

Global Guilt

To be honest, I don't know how much my travels in Africa helped anyone there. Short-term mission trips can be controversial, and according to one school of thought, it's better to just directly donate the money you'd otherwise spend traveling. I do think there's some merit in visiting the same way you would visit a sick friend in the hospital. Certainly you could send money or flowers, but being present is really a sweet gesture, and the children in Sierra Leone were genuinely over the moon to spend time with us. Still, I can't say for sure how long the excitement lasted once we left. I don't know how much their lives were improved by our trip, but I can say without a doubt that mine was changed forever.

When I returned home, I experienced random bursts of tears for several months. They were not outbursts of pity toward Africa, but rather a strange stirring resembling the nostalgia you get from missing your own childhood, mixed with the rude awakening of seeing your own culture and home in a completely new light. All I could think was,

Why is so much of the focus in America on buying the biggest house you can and filling it with stuff? Buying all the clothes you can at huge buildings dedicated to spending money, called malls, and filling an enormous closet with as many clothes as you can (or can't) afford? It felt like I was shedding a layer of skin, or bursting the tiny little bubble I had been living in all my life. I was mourning having lived in the Matrix for so long. Children who lived in a tiny village in Africa with no utilities were free from all this "stuff" and so happy without any of it. And here I was, in the suburbs, shackled in the invisible chains of modern conveniences and societal expectations to keep up with the Joneses.

I've always been cognizant that caring for others is of the utmost importance. We had a cast of characters at our dinner table growing up, like Esther, an elderly neighbor who had recently lost her husband. My mom took her under her wing, made her dinner, and helped clean her house. Anyone who needed a meal was welcome in our home. And volunteer work outside the home was heartily encouraged and a big part of my life from as young as I can remember. From volunteering at hospitals in middle school, to implementing a new volunteer program in college, to serving at a local food pantry in Boston in my early twenties, I have always been very passionate about serving others.

But Africa changed things. Whereas before I was happy fitting in volunteer work and monetary donations where it made sense in my daily life, now all my daily activities seemed frivolous, and I wanted to spend 100 percent of my time helping others. Shouldn't I lay absolutely all of it down, and go out and make a difference?

After our mission trip to Africa, our team formed a small group and met weekly. We studied the Bible and read several books together, including *Radical: Taking Back Your Faith from the American Dream* by David Platt. The message of that book, as you may have surmised by the title, is to get really radical about your life and helping others. Platt believes that we should all sell our modern homes, move overseas, and spend our time helping those in need, much like it says in Matthew 19:21.

In so many ways the book jibed with how I was feeling post-Africa. I was already rethinking the pursuit of wealth and the often me-centered culture in our country. But *Radical* also helped me personally determine where to draw that line in my life. The "radical" thoughts laid out in the book were similar to my post-Africa thoughts, and perhaps Platt and I were taking it a little too far. Here's why.

Realization #1: Sometimes There's Shame in Our Pity

Have you ever experienced the "people across the globe are in need" type of guilt like I have? This is the guilt you feel when you pick up a pair of jeans and all you can think about are the kids in third-world countries who are living without running water. It's a real thing, it haunts me, and maybe it haunts you too.

But let's imagine for a moment a woman across town in her sprawling mansion. She feels this pain for others, so she sobs on her bed because she can't bear the thought of buying another Louis Vuitton, when you, across town, are living in your middle-class house and can't afford all-organic food or that new BMW. She just can't stomach it! Stop it right there, right? Because you'd be like, "Um, I'm okay, thanks!"

What feels so off about these examples is that they place the person being pitied in a "less than" position. Melody Fletcher, author of *Deliberate Receiving: Finally, the Universe Makes Some Freakin' Sense!*, poses these insightful questions that illustrate this situation:

> What if instead of feeling badly for people who have less than you, you brightened their day with a smile and a joke? What if you treated them as equals, rather than people who need to be pitied and are somehow failing? What if you stopped judging people by how

much money or stuff they have and just connected with who they really are? What if you became the one person in their lives who actually saw . . . their potential, believed in them and let them know it? How do you think that would feel to them?[1]

Loving and helping those in need should certainly be the focus of our lives, but seeing others as "less than" can actually hurt more than it helps by denying the other person's power and disempowering them of their ability to help themselves. Trust me when I say that you might be feeling selfless in that moment—and you are absolutely right to be considerate of others—but the men, women, and children I met in Africa would have been puzzled by thoughts of not buying the jeans for their "sake." The negative emotions of pity or guilt aren't helping anyone with anything. (So cut it out!) Sometimes we unknowingly cast shame in our charity, and it's important to know the difference.

Realization #2: It's Not About You

A misinformed idea that often goes hand in hand with viewing others as "less than" is assuming that we are the ones who must help. Sure, stepping up to help can seem others-focused at the time. But assuming that we have all the answers can be infinitely more self-focused in some ways, making it about "us" and not about the people we are helping at all.

In her 2014 article for the Huffington Post, "The Problem with Little White Girls, Boys and Voluntourism," Pippa Biddle writes:

---

[1] Melody Fletcher, "Do You Feel Guilty About Having More Money Than Others?," *Deliberate Receiving blog!*, November 20, 2011, http://www.deliberateblog.com/2011/11/20/do-you-feel-guilty-about-having-more-money-than-others-part-2.

I am a 5'4" white girl who can carry bags of moderately heavy stuff, horse around with kids, attempt to teach a class, tell the story of how I found myself (with accompanying PowerPoint) to a few thousand people and not much else.

Some might say that that's enough. That as long as I go to X country with an open mind and a good heart I'll leave at least one child so uplifted and emboldened by my short stay that they will, for years, think of me every morning.

[But] I don't want a little girl in Ghana, or Sri Lanka, or Indonesia to think of me when she wakes up each morning. I don't want her to thank me for her education or medical care or new clothes. Even if I am providing the funds to get the ball rolling, I want her to think about her teacher, community leader, or mother. I want her to have a hero who she can relate to—who looks like her, is part of her culture, speaks her language, and who she might bump into on the way to school one morning.

Pippa makes several good points. First, we all have a specific skill set, so trying to solve any and all world problems is probably not based in reality; certainly we don't possess the skill or know-how to fix every type of problem. Second, we may try to or wish we could "leave our mark," even when it's not always appropriate, like in the example she gives, and when a local hero would make infinitely more sense.

This phenomenon, that we must always be the ones to save the children or solve problems in foreign countries, is what's widely known as the "savior complex." Perpetrated in popular movies (in everything from *Dances with Wolves* to *The Blind Side*), and even in our foreign policies and school curricula, we've learned that we (often meaning Americans, but this could certainly be applied to anyone) are portrayed as, and thus taught to be, the ones who step in and save the day.

We certainly don't want to find ourselves in a vicious cycle of "no, you go" when no one steps in to help because everyone just assumes someone else will. But we also do more damage than good when we believe that we must be the ones to step in every single time. It implies that we think that "we" (however our collective group is defined) are the only ones who are competent enough to solve the world's problems. It also removes God as the general of this battle, when He should always assume that position of honor. We may step in as His helper and as a good soldier from time to time, running to the scene to provide aid, but putting ourselves at the helm can result in making it entirely too much about us.

Realization #3: Sometimes We Fix the Wrong Things in the Wrong Way

When we take control of saving the world, we often fail in one very profound way by trying to fix the wrong things. We may rush in to save the day before taking time to listen and understand the needs of those we are trying to help. For example, we may want to "fix" a village in a third-world country because they don't have TVs or cell phones. But upon further examination we realize that they actually don't want technology at all because they see it as a barrier to a deeper connection and a togetherness that they cherish with their families and neighborhood. Earlier I mentioned children not having running water as a tension point while buying jeans, but during my time in Africa I found taking bucket baths to actually be a quite an efficient (and even enjoyable) way to bathe. While access to clean water is critical, maybe the lack of a modern shower and running water aren't things we necessarily need to "fix."

The solutions we often wish to implement are centered on our own experiences (like the desire for a hot shower), but our experiences are not necessarily suited to someone else's problems. Take TOMS shoes, for example. The company founder, Blake Mycoskie, identified a pressing issue: kids without shoes were stepping on things, getting sick, and even dying from the ensuing infections. His solution was to start a shoe company with a "one for one" concept—for every pair of shoes purchased, TOMS donates a pair to someone in need. Clearly kids getting sick from stepping on things is a very serious problem, and finding ways to solve it is commendable on many levels.

But giving away free shoes may not always be the best solution: because now a kid is wearing free shoes versus granting parents the dignity of an income so that they can afford to buy the shoes themselves. Giving away free things may affect the entire economy of that country, taking away potential jobs from locals who make shoes. (There's more on how our donations sometimes harm third-world countries in chapter 9.) Not to mention that here in the United States people may wear their TOMS shoes as a badge of honor, but overseas, it can be embarrassing or shameful to wear things that were free. It's not that the recipients aren't grateful, but perhaps they aren't proud of wearing the shoes, either. They may choose to go barefoot over wearing the donated shoes as a result, and thus we find ourselves back at the original problem: barefoot kids stepping on things and hurting themselves.

Or consider our friend Jordan, who recently traveled to Haiti to build a new school. He recounted how each day he went to work constructing a building, while twenty or so local Haitian men who were in dire need of jobs sat staring at him, wishing they could work. We may identify that Haiti needs a new building, so we fly down there and give them a building. But they see that they need a building, and wish that we would give them the training and resources so that they can build it themselves. Certainly both Blake's and Jordan's hearts are in the right place, and it's commendable of them to step in and help. But we may not always correctly identify the problems we see, and the solutions we apply to them may not really be what's best after all.

Realization #4: Choice Equals Dignity

No matter how disenfranchised or down and out someone may be, one thing remains true about the human spirit: we desire freedom and the ability to make choices for ourselves. During my trip to Sierra Leone, I purchased a huge stack of beaded bracelets from a local artisan. I handed them out to my team members and (with permission) gave them to the women and children that we were working with. I bought a big stack so that everyone could have one—I was being really diplomatic by making sure there was enough to go around. Right? Wrong.

Our beautiful cook didn't want one. She told me that if she did wear a bracelet like that, she'd want a big stack to make a style statement. It's hard for me to admit this line of thinking, but I hope it helps drive home a point: at first, my reaction to her rejection was, She doesn't want this free thing?! But she has no bracelets on at all! Why wouldn't she want it?

Surely, this conversation about bracelets happened while she cooked over a fire in a hut made of branches, with no access to running water or electricity—but making choices about her style was still important to her. Why wouldn't it be? She's a human with personal taste and opinions, just like anyone else.

Consider the capital city Kinshasa, tucked far into the jungle of the Democratic Republic of the Congo. Poverty is rampant there, but the area is also well known for local men, called Sapeurs, who dress in elaborate, dandy outfits that are completely over the top and stand out in stark contrast. Maybe this seems backward to us, because in our American culture personal style is often prioritized last and only explored in situations where there are excessive resources. But clothing can actually be an important piece of the bigger picture for a neighborhood or region, for the dignity it provides the wearer via the freedom of personal expression. Sometimes we have a bad habit of giving away our junk, or offering up any little thing, and expecting people to love it, but the ability to make choices often far outweighs any potential allure of "free stuff."

Realization #5: Our Blessings Don't Limit Someone Else's Blessings

When my husband and I bought our first home, it was a long, tedious process spanning more than a year. During the same season, he was the lead advocate for the Rethink Homelessness campaign, which raises awareness and provides resources for the homeless population in Central Florida. We were buried deep in conversations about subway tiles and the size of the master suite. On the streets of downtown Orlando, he was buried deep in conversations about what it's like to not even have a home at all.

His time with the homeless helped us keep our purchasing decision in perspective. (Is stainless steel really a deal breaker? Probably not.) But we absolutely still bought a house, and our decision to do so was not to the detriment of my husband's homeless friends.

Even though it can sometimes feel like blessings are limited—that if we take one thing for ourselves, like a few minutes and some money to buy a new dress, we are doing something to hurt others—it's not a matter of "I buy myself something, and someone else goes without." It just doesn't work that way. Sometimes we tell ourselves it works that way, and that the money we're using could go to charity, but unless we literally take those dollar bills and walk over to a donation bucket and put them there instead, the decision to buy the jeans or not does not usually affect our charitable giving. Either we're buying the jeans or we're not, and the idea of giving to charity is an entirely separate decision that's made at a later time.

Think of it this way: If you're in line at 7-Eleven to buy coffee and you see a homeless person, do you put down the coffee and give them the two dollars instead? Unlikely. Do you buy them a coffee as well? Absolutely, or you may stop and give them a couple dollars on the way out in addition to buying yourself coffee. But ultimately buying the coffee is not going to mean someone else goes without. In reality the two decisions are almost never related. (This is also where having both a clothing budget and a charity budget comes into play, which we will discuss in detail in chapter 9.)

My husband's homeless friends were at total ease with this principle. They regularly asked about our home-buying process and how we were doing, and there wasn't any instance where it was uncomfortable or anyone seemed jealous. In fact, it was quite the opposite. His friends were genuinely interested in our search and were so happy for us when we finally found a home. There was never any desire for us not to have a home: they just wanted one too! And they knew that just because we were buying a home, it wouldn't mean that someone else was going without. There is not a limited, one-in, one-out principle when it comes to blessings. It's not on any one person's shoulders to spread blessings, and there is absolutely enough blessing to go around for everyone.

Realization #6: Your Blessings Multiply into More Blessings

Now that we have a home and a place to lay our heads to rest at night, my husband and I are able to help the homeless more than we ever could before. While we were deep in our home search, we were living out of suitcases and struggling with the most basic issues of lodging ourselves, so it was harder to help others. But with our basic needs now covered, we're able think about helping others in new and different ways.

Which illustrates this next point: your blessings can multiply into more blessings. Our new home is not only a place that provides us with shelter and stability, but we also use it to provide for others' needs by hosting events for our church, for nonprofits, and for fundraising. The same could be said of a new outfit: it can empower and aid you in presenting yourself to a group of wealthy donors or politicians, which in turn benefits causes you care deeply about. You could be called upon to address the United Nations on behalf of a marginalized group, for example, but doing so in rags does not necessarily benefit your cause (unless, of course, your mode of dress is part of the message). A home or new clothing could be seen as a selfish purchase, but it's also possible to use your purchases as a tool to help even more people on an even larger scale than you could without them.

For example, if your neighbor needed a car, you could give them yours, but then you would lose the ability to get to work, pick up your kids from school, and provide transportation to anyone else who needs a ride. If your friend has an accident and becomes paralyzed, you could commiserate and confine yourself to a wheelchair, but it would limit your ability to take care of yourself as well as help them get around. Your blessings, like your car, your clothes, your heath, and anything else, only multiply into more blessings when used for a higher purpose.

Realization #7: We Have Different Callings

The author of *Radical* felt personally called to answer Matthew 19:21. His family sold their house and committed themselves full time to helping people in need. I believe for him it was absolutely the right thing to do (but either way, it wouldn't be my place to say). I also believe that we each have our own individual callings that are unique. I don't think Jesus was telling everyone to sell their possessions in Matthew 19:21 when he said, "If you want to be perfect, go, sell your possessions and give to the poor, and you will have treasure in heaven. Then come, follow me" (NIV).

For starters, Jesus was speaking to one specific person in that passage. As any good doctor would, Jesus prescribed things that were customized to the ailment at hand. The man in question was "very wealthy" and as Jesus would go on to tell him, "It is easier for a camel to go through the eye of a needle than for someone who is rich to enter the kingdom of God." So in this man's case, off-loading his possessions was wise advice. Jesus also uses the phrase "if you want to be perfect" because the man was already following the Ten Commandments and wanted to know how he could do even more. ("What still do I lack?")

Certainly, beyond living a penniless existence, there are great callings and vocations in life, as we discussed in detail in chapter 2. A calling to play piano, create works of art, author cookbooks, or even write a fashion blog is not any lesser than the calling of a pastor or a doctor (just different), and ultimately we can honor God no matter where we are in life, and no matter our calling.

Sometimes, though, the injustice of the world feels truly unbearable, and when we are given a really "good" station in life, it can be tough to wonder why we are blessed with such a fulfilling career, great wealth, or a loving family.

Listen to the way A-list actress Angelina Jolie addressed this tension so poignantly in her acceptance speech for the Jean Hersholt Humanitarian Award in 2013:

> I have never understood why some people are lucky enough to be born with the chance that I had—with this path in life. And why across the world, there's a woman just like me, with the same abilities and the same desires, the same work ethic and love for her family, who would most likely make better films and better speeches. Only she sits in a refugee camp. And she had no voice. She worries about what her children will eat, how to keep them safe, and if they'll ever return home. I don't know why this is my life and that's hers . . . But I will do as my mother asked, and

I will do the best I can with this life, and to be of use
[to others].[2]

Should Angelina Jolie never have pursued acting? Should she have
instead spent all her time volunteering at a soup kitchen? Because it
really makes a lot more sense, to me, that she is the award-winning
actress that she is. Her acting talent may not save a child's life in the
moment, but she has absolutely shown it can be used as a tool for
change. Her celebrity has allowed her a powerful platform, to shine a
light on the plight of refugees around the world[3]. She has traveled to
desperate places, with the media watching, to publicize how people
have been forced from their homes, and she has worked hard to influence policies and programs that help refugees. I would argue that she
has made a huge difference, much more so than if she weren't Angelina
Jolie, the actress. She has compelled others to commit time and money
to her cause. She has witnessed things we may never be able to see firsthand, and she brought back that news to us.

As a teacher or a construction worker, you may not have the same
celebrity as Angelina Jolie, but you can influence the children in your
classroom, your coworkers, and the people in your community to love
others like Jesus would, and to care about issues that seem so far away,
like sex trafficking. You can use your hard-earned money to donate to
the amazing organizations that know how to solve problems like economic turmoil and the conflicts leading to refugee displacement.

---

2   Pippa Biddle, "The Problem with Little White Girls, Boys and
     Voluntourism," *HuffPost* (blog), April 25, 2014, http://www
     .huffingtonpost.com/pippa-biddle/little-white-girls-voluntourism_b
     _4834574.html.
3   Stephanie Vatz, "Why America Stopped Making Its Own Clothes," *The
     Lowdown*, KQED News, May 24, 2013, https://ww2.kqed.org/lowdown
     /2013/05/24/madeinamerica.

If Angelina Jolie ever feels her heart is telling her to sell her belongings and move overseas and help those refugees in a different way, then she should absolutely do it. And if that happens to me, I will answer the call too. But I think some of us were made to fight in the trenches overseas, and some of us weren't. Or sometimes we go for a season and then we come back. I am so thankful for those men and women who are currently soldiers, missionaries, and pastors. But there are many of us called to work in the arts and be hairdressers, actors, and musicians too. (I'd say my calling falls in this second category.) And like Angelina Jolie, we can use all of those resources we gain when we shine with the talents and in the place we've been given.

Mom Guilt and Others-Centered Exhaustion

Realization #8: You Can't Pour from an Empty Cup

Perhaps my trip to Africa and the resulting reverse culture shock I experienced doesn't resonate with you. Perhaps it's not people overseas that you think of when you hit the mall. Rather, it's hard for you to enjoy fashion or art because spending time and money on yourself feels like it takes time and money away from someone much closer to home—your family and children. Maybe you can't possibly imagine buying yourself jeans with all of the groceries you need to buy and the clothes your kids need. And the kids always need it way more than you do—or so you tell yourself.

That feeling that you're not doing enough for your children or family is called "mom guilt." It's the basic principle of "I have so many things I need to do for others, I can't possibly think about caring for myself," and it's a pretty universal feeling, especially for women. It seems to be intimately connected to the framework of our feminine nature.

There's something about our essence that causes us to be concerned with making sure everyone around us is taken care of at all times.

I think this innate urge to nurture and mother is a beautiful thing, and God put those desires in our heart for a reason. Many of us know the blessing that is the mother figure, who sends us care packages at college, frets that we aren't eating enough or wearing warm enough sweaters, and fusses over every last detail to make sure we are okay—whether it comes from our birth mother, surrogate mother, or a caring friend.

But there can be a darker side to that mothering nature if we take it too far. Because, as women, if we never take care of ourselves—by getting enough sleep and exercise, and even buying ourselves clothes—it can lead to others-centered exhaustion: where you're so empty that you have nothing left to give to anyone else, and when you're so worried about everyone else and their problems that you forget to take care of yourself, and you suffer for it.

I'm a recovering others-aholic myself. When I started blogging in 2010, I had a very passionate others-centered focus. I was motivated to blog by a deep desire to make a difference in fashion journalism and to help others with their practical style issues. As my readership increased, though, a problem emerged. I eventually had more questions and requests than one human can possibly answer. The emails piled up and the ones I never answered still haunt me like a ghost to this day. (The "ghost of emails past due.")

In my others-centered focus, I also found myself way too concerned with making everyone happy. Which is incredibly difficult when everyone wants different things. One person would ask me for more outfits with flats, and in the same comment thread someone else would be saying they never wanted to see me post flat shoes again. (Perhaps you can relate at dinnertime, when everyone in your family is being super-picky and wants different types of foods!) I nearly drove myself crazy trying to please everyone.

I felt like I had the weight of the world on my shoulders. I wasn't sleeping enough or eating right, and emotionally I was beyond drained. A friend asked me for something and I snapped. I couldn't take another person needing something from me! It was too much! Why couldn't everyone leave me alone! Really helpful attitude when you're in the business of helping people, right? Oh boy!

The moral of this story is that you simply can't pour from an empty cup. When you don't take any time for self-care, you are useless in helping anyone. You're too tired to think about what your kids need, or your neighbors down the street who got into an accident, or your friend who is a new mom if you don't "selfishly" carve out time for yourself to sleep. You're too hungry to think about problems in third-world countries if you don't "selfishly" take time out to enjoy and savor a nice, delicious meal from time to time. You may feel too threadbare to host a fundraiser or attend a charity event when you don't take time out to "selfishly" enjoy a trip to the store for a new outfit. And the list goes on.

Our pastor recommended a book on this topic, *When People are Big and God is Small: Overcoming Peer Pressure, Codependency, and the Fear of Man*, and it was instrumental in helping me move forward on this issue. A lot of times those feelings of wanting to help are linked to very real fears, and people-pleasing is a very real condition. That book and a lot of prayer helped me realize my focus was entirely in the wrong place. Why was I so wrapped up in serving everyone? I needed to make God my number one priority. Having just one master (God) helped me decrease the clutter of so many voices wanting different things from me. Instead of hearing a rushing symphony of the millions of people in need across the world, or the handful of voices of your children and spouse at home, you can focus on only one voice guiding your path.

We're told on airplanes that in the event of an emergency you should secure your own oxygen mask before helping others, and in nature, the lioness eats before her lion cubs, and for good reason. The lioness must keep her energy and nutrition up so that she is able to continue caring for her cubs and providing more food. And you can't help anyone with their oxygen mask if you're passed out from not getting enough oxygen yourself. It may seem selfish on the surface, but you absolutely cannot help others if you don't help yourself first. Hitting the recharge button and feeling free to enjoy traveling, spa days, a new wardrobe, or a nice meal, are crucially important to refilling our souls. When done right, self-care allows us to help others more, not less.

Realization #9: Get More Done in Less Time with a Sabbath.

I was blogging for seven days a week for over four years. I'm a classic overachiever, and this type of work ethic appeals to me in some ways, but I also physically couldn't keep up—it was just too much. I reluctantly made the switch to blogging six days a week, and ironically, my revenue and production actually went up, not down! When you abuse the goose (yourself, your body, your mind) you will not produce any golden eggs. And it turns out that I was able to be more productive in those six days than I ever was in seven days. God rested on the seventh day in the creation story, and in Exodus 20:8–21 and several other places in the Bible it commands us to do the same. I'm not great with math, but somehow less time spent actually equals more productivity in many cases.

> Remember the Sabbath day by keeping it holy. Six days you shall labor and do all your work, but the seventh day is a sabbath to the Lord your God. On it you shall not do any work, neither you, nor your son or daughter, nor your male or female servant, nor your animals, nor any foreigner residing in your towns. For in six days the Lord made the heavens and the earth, the sea, and all that is in them, but he rested on the

seventh day. Therefore the Lord blessed the Sabbath day and made it holy. (NIV)

If we try to give all our time to anything—whether it's blogging, being a mom, or working with the poor—our productivity will suffer. If we take a restorative break now and then—to rest, to enjoy art, or to do something kind for ourselves, whether that means, for you, buying a new outfit or spending a day at the spa—we often find we're even more effective.

Realization #10: Self-Care Is Setting a Good Example

My friend Stacey is a powerhouse. She has done some admirable things in her career, including creating and hosting a small business conference here in Orlando. As we walked out of the conference together, I was thinking how hard it must've been to accomplish this feat with two small kids at home. And, sensing she might be feeling some "mom guilt" for spending so much time away from home in order to host the conference, I said to her, "You know, I think it's an amazing example you are setting for your kids, especially your daughter, that women can do anything they set their minds to and can make such an impact in the community."

My mom stayed home with me, which also had incredible merits and benefits during my childhood. There's really no wrong way to go about it in my book. But my point is this: if you do what makes your heart happy—whether that's being a powerhouse conference-throwing career woman, or taking some time to enjoy your love of crafting or fashion, or heading to the gym to exercise—then your kids will see that. Your own accomplishments and self-care sets the example for the self-care you want to see your children embrace as well.

Beth, a mom and contributor to Knoxville Moms Blog in Tennessee, shares her thoughts on setting an example for her kids:

I don't always want to be in yoga pants at the grocery store, ya know? Sometimes I am totally that mom. But other times I try to put myself together because when I feel good about myself when I walk out the door—it sets the tone for the day. When you wake up refreshed your child feeds off of it and other people do too. There's a blogger who wants to teach her daughter looks don't matter by not combing her own or her daughter's hair. I can't help but think we have some responsibility to teach our children about these things, though. I feel good about what I'm doing and the example I set for my daughter.

As we discussed in chapters 5 and 6, self-esteem is a crucial part of our human experience, and we know from chapter 3 that clothes are an unavoidable topic and important to our role within society. When we find a balance in our clothing and our outer appearance, we can be sure that our kiddos are watching—and learning. When viewed this way, self-care is tough to label as selfish, because it's actually helping our kids. Our self-care urges them to participate in their own self-care and can actually be a form of healthy parenting.

Realization #11: The Guilt Goes Both Ways

"I'm sorry." The words escaped my mouth before I could stop myself. I was grocery shopping with zero makeup and wearing my sweaty post-gym clothes, and a woman who reads my blog stopped me to say hello. So of course my instinct was to apologize, right? Because not being dressed up or looking presentable in public is something we should feel guilty about? (Huge eye roll.) Why do we do this to ourselves? I struggle with feeling guilty for spending time and money on makeup and cute clothes so much that I created an entire blog and career around it. So why, then, when I'm not wearing makeup or cute clothes, do I also feel guilty? It's as if I can't win.

This type of guilt, I'm told, is very common for moms. And, in general, magazines and the media are constantly advising us to dress up for our husbands and jobs and to put more effort into our appearance. You might look down at yourself six months after having a baby and not remember the last time you weren't wearing stretchy clothes covered in spit-up, then feel a twinge of guilt for not having started a program to lose the baby weight yet. But when we take the time to get dressed or spend money on our appearances, then we are also faced with guilt and the question posed in this chapter: Is fashion selfish?

Recognizing that the guilt that tries to cut us both ways plays a central role in answering this question. Because when we view our style decisions within this larger framework, we realize it's actually impossible for shopping and getting dressed to be inherently selfish. If we find that on the other side, abstaining from fashion completely yields the exact same result—heaps of guilt—then the answer, logically, must lie somewhere in the middle. The existence of one type of guilt negates the other. (It's also, if I may be frank, absolute insanity.)

If you're going to feel guilty about doing one thing, then you shouldn't also guilt yourself for doing the opposite. Understanding the dynamic as it plays out on both sides helps us go forward with the confidence that it's not one or the other—that fashion can't be flat-out selfish—and that we're on a journey of finding the right balance for us and our families. Moms or not, we cannot be expected to be both.

Putting an End to Guilt

I regularly fight the urge to wear my fashion guilt as a badge of honor. I may feel like a jerk, for example, if my blessings don't come with a huge, heaping side dish of feeling guilty about people who don't have what I have, or if the time and money I spend on clothes feels like I'm taking away that time and money from someone else. But it's time to snap out of it, because not only is that line of thinking false, but all that time spent on guilt can be the problem itself.

Melody Fletcher, author of *Deliberate Receiving*, puts it so well:

> Your guilt does nothing to help anyone. Seriously, how is your feeling horrible going to help others feed their families? How are your pity and empathy going to raise Africans out of poverty, provide proper shelter to children living in Shantytowns, or give the homeless guy a place to plug in his iPad? The truth is, you can't feel badly enough to make them feel better, and you can't get poor enough to make them richer.[4]

When we talk about global responsibility and helping our neighbors, it's a very complex subject, and I certainly don't have all the answers. I just think that when we've done our due diligence, when we've put in the time volunteering or donated a reasonable amount of money, then we absolutely can and should feel free to buy the jeans.

Because ultimately we can't control the financial or emotional situations of the world. We can't solve world problems with our guilt and our groveling. And if we attempt to make ourselves poor in order to make someone else rich, then the result will just be two poor people instead of one. While we are absolutely charged to care about the situations of those around us, to put others before ourselves at times and to be willing to help, it can actually do more harm than good when we

---

4   Melody Fletcher, "Do You Feel Guilty About Having More Money Than Others?," *Deliberate Receiving blog!*, November 20, 2011, http://www.deliberateblog.com/2011/11/20/do-you-feel-guilty-about-having-more-money-than-others-part-2.

commit to others 100 percent of the time and don't set aside any time and money for ourselves.

The only thing we can truly control is our own situation. And to help others, we must first get to a place where that's possible. We are most effective in helping others, and honoring the "golden rule" of putting others before ourselves, when we are operating from a place where our spiritual, physical, and emotional needs are provided for. (And sometimes, that even includes clothes!)

Chapter 8

How Much Money Should I Spend on Fashion?

> The sheen of silk, draped across a mannequin. Oh, the smell of new Italian leather shoes . . . The rush you feel when you swipe your [credit] card. And it's approved. And it all belongs to you![1]

That's the fictional Rebecca Bloomwood in the movie *Confessions of a Shopaholic* talking. Bloomwood (played by Isla Fisher) personifies all of the stereotypes of a "fashionista" rolled into one. She waits in absurdly long lines for designer sample sales, she can't walk past a store window display without stopping in "just to look," she dresses in head-to-toe bright colors and all the latest trends, and she keeps an emergency credit card in a block of ice in her freezer.

So often when we picture a woman shopping for clothing or your typical fashion blogger, we picture Rebecca Bloomwood. Certainly many of us, myself included, have had moments of being drawn to a

---

1 "*Confessions of a Shopaholic* Script – Dialogue Transcript," Script-O -Rama.com, accessed June 11, 2017, http://www.script-o-rama.com /movie_scripts/a1/confessions-of-a-shopaholic-script.html.

window display or getting really excited about a deal we just scored. Maybe we use shopping to relax or reward ourselves, or maybe we get a little carried away and buy something we later regret. But Bloomwood takes it to a whole other level. She has a full-fledged shopping addiction with very real consequences, like losing her job, ruining her credit, and putting a strain on her relationship with her parents. She's just a character in a movie, but shopping addictions are not just for the big screen. Take this real-life example:

> Amanda was a police detective in a large Midwestern city. As a compulsive buyer, she shopped three times a day on eBay and her house was overflowing with clothes, books, and magazines.
>
> Amanda couldn't focus on her new husband and lied to him about shopping. She felt like she was "dumbing [herself] down" with her constant preoccupation with purchasing. Her former interests, like social and environmental causes, went by the wayside in favor of focusing on buying things.[2]

It can be easy to remove ourselves from the "addicted to shopping" category, as most of us probably don't struggle at that level. We don't put ourselves in debt, and our shopping doesn't negatively affect our relationships. When we compare ourselves to Amanda or Rebecca Bloomwood, we instantly feel like we're in good shape. But while we may not be anywhere in shopaholic territory, it's still possible that we allow money to control us in different, sometimes sneakier, ways.

---

2 Molly Triffin, "How to Quit Shopping Addiction," *DailyWorth* (blog), December 2, 2015, https://www.dailyworth.com/posts/4021-how-to-quit-shopping-addiction.

While overspending can be an addiction or a fault, so can saving too much, being far too frugal, or not having a giving spirit. And while some of us operate under a fear of poverty or a fear of wealth (or, in my case, a little bit of both simultaneously!), when we worry too much about either end of the spectrum, that preoccupation becomes a problem itself.

Money is a touchy but vastly important topic. The Bible has approximately five hundred verses on prayer, five hundred verses on faith, and more than two thousand on money. It's the subject of more than half of the parables that Jesus tells in the New Testament.[3] Certainly, an unhealthy relationship with money can lead us into dangerous sin, and shopping is an easy place to get into hot water, so it's an important topic to address truthfully in our lives.

So what does a healthy relationship with money look like? What are some common issues with money, and how do they manifest in our faith and in our spending? And what are practical steps for moving forward with a budget and financial plan for enjoying fashion within the context of our faith?

Frugal to a Fault: The Fear of Poverty

I come from a long line of farmers, factory workers, and truck drivers on both sides of my family. My father's parents struggled greatly through the Great Depression, and as a result they were incredibly frugal. My grandmother, I'm told, was no fun to bake with because she could empty a mixing bowl so efficiently there was no batter left to lick. My father's money values were shaped by them, and he followed in their footsteps, wearing shoes and shirts with giant gaping holes in them

---

3 "Statistic: Jesus' Teachings on Money," PreachingToday, December 1996, http://www.preachingtoday.com/illustrations/1996/december/410.html.

around the house, and driving the most embarrassing rusted-out bright orange truck during my teen years. Every bit of energy consumption, like turning on the lights, was closely monitored in our house. I was only allowed to order the cheapest food on the menu on the rare occasions we ate at restaurants, and we took maybe three vacations total while I was growing up.

My dad was the first to go to college in our family, and he paid for everything in cash, even our cars and house. He purchased the land for our house first, in cash. Years later, after saving more money, he began construction by renting a backhoe and digging the hole for the foundation himself. He worked weekends for years to complete the house, doing as much as he could alone, and paying plumbers, electricians, and the like along the way with the money he had saved. I have so many childhood memories of our house in various phases of construction. I would help him by doing small jobs, like sweeping, while pretending I was "swabbing the ship deck."

My dad's frugal ways and his all-cash policy often embarrassed me or frustrated me as a teenager, so I attempted to approach money in a bit more of a balanced way. In college, I worked part time so that I could take trips to places I had never been, like New York City and Miami, and I used a small amount of my earnings to explore personal expression through clothes. But many of those frugal tendencies that I grew up around were not as easy to beat as I had originally thought. Ultimately, I found myself in my early twenties struggling to spend money on clothes, even when I really needed them for work, and even when I had plenty of money with which to buy them.

In chapter 3, I told the story of how I lost a dream job because I was too frugal to buy an appropriate outfit for the interview. And even after I bought a suit and landed a good job, I found myself repeatedly in uncomfortable work situations where I was not dressed appropriately, or I was freezing to death in cold Boston winters because I didn't have warm-enough clothes. I was struggling with the messaging I'd received from a young age that clothing purchases were frivolous in nature and essentially off-limits, and that it was far wiser to keep your money in a savings account out of a fear of poverty (which was rooted in my grandparents' struggling during the Great Depression—it's amazing how far messaging like that can travel in a family).

As I mentioned before, that guilt I experienced every time I bought something, even when I really needed it, is one thing that led me to start a fashion blog many years ago. I know my blog can be easily misunderstood as the musings of your stereotypical Rebecca Bloomwood type. For example, a reader recently commented along the lines of "You've been shopping and spending so much money lately, I'm concerned!" On my blog, it can very much *appear* that I spend gobs of time and money on clothes, I'll give the concerned reader that much. But my blog is about clothes, which is only a tiny little fraction of my life. I enjoy adding new things to my closet for sure, but then again shopping hardly even appeals to me on a personal level, and it's only occasionally fun—I'd certainly survive if I never set foot in a mall again!

Clothing for me is also not so much about how I look—I'm just as happy in sweats and no makeup. For me, fashion is an art form, a creative expression and a deeper calling of my heart, than of a daily practice. My blog was very much born out of wanting to challenge myself in this area, to put more effort into this passion for creating outfits, and to share the journey along the way. And in doing so it unearthed a creative zest and enjoyment in experimenting with clothes that I had not yet fully realized. When I do the "am I spending too much money on my outer appearance?" check, I feel confident that I pass with flying colors, because that draw to spend a lot of money on clothing or even look put-together most days is just simply not there for me.

But what if I'm not really passing as well as I think I am? Am I fooling myself into thinking that I'm in control of money because I'm not interested in overspending or wearing a bunch of fancy clothes? Is it still possible to sin when it comes to fashion and money by controlling money in a different way? What if I'm sinning in the other direction?

Because I'd like to propose that on both sides of the scale—whether we are talking about overspending or hoarding money—we are guilty of loving money too much. When we overspend, we crave money for the next shopping spree we can go on. We seek money for the emotional high and become dependent on the rush of dopamine that is released into our brains when we shop. On the other side of the equation, when we are far too frugal, we crave controlling money a different way. We want our money in our bank account where we can keep an eye on it. We are too fearful of letting it go, even to the detriment of not landing the job or not helping a neighbor in need because we wish to keep money under our own control.

Frugality ⟵⟶ Overspending

I am personally much more prone to the sin of frugality, or hoarding money out of fear of not having enough. I'm like a page out of my dad's own book, the way I scrimp and save, even when I'm not necessarily in a position that I need to. Sometimes I am the servant who receives one bag of gold from his master and buries it in the ground, as in the Parable of the Talents (also known as Parable of Bags of Gold) in Matthew 25:14–29.

> Again, it will be like a man going on a journey, who called his servants and entrusted his wealth to them. To one he gave five bags of gold, to another two bags, and to another one bag, each according to his ability. Then he went on his journey. The man who had received five bags of gold went at once and put his money to work and gained five bags more. So also, the one with two bags of gold gained two more. But the

man who had received one bag went off, dug a hole in the ground and hid his master's money.

After a long time the master of those servants returned and settled accounts with them. The man who had received five bags of gold brought the other five. "Master," he said, "you entrusted me with five bags of gold. See, I have gained five more."

His master replied, "Well done, good and faithful servant! You have been faithful with a few things; I will put you in charge of many things. Come and share your master's happiness!"

The man with two bags of gold also came. "Master," he said, "you entrusted me with two bags of gold; see, I have gained two more."

His master replied, "Well done, good and faithful servant! You have been faithful with a few things; I will put you in charge of many things. Come and share your master's happiness!"

Then the man who had received one bag of gold came. "Master," he said, "I knew that you are a hard man, harvesting where you have not sown and gathering where you have not scattered seed. So I was afraid and went out and hid your gold in the ground. See, here is what belongs to you."

His master replied, "You wicked, lazy servant! So you knew that I harvest where I have not sown and gather where I have not scattered seed? Well then, you should have put my money on deposit with the bankers, so that when I returned I would have received it back with interest.

"So take the bag of gold from him and give it to the one who has ten bags. For whoever has will be given more, and they will have an abundance. Whoever does not have, even what they have will be taken from them." (NIV)

One interpretation of this parable is that Jesus is advising us to be a good steward of money by investing it wisely. Interestingly, we don't see a materialistic Rebecca Bloomwood type who goes out and fruitlessly spends money in this example. This parable is devoid of that type of money sin altogether. Instead it focuses on the other sin—of being too frugal, and keeping money to ourselves. There are two servants who invest wisely—one with far more bags of gold than the other—to illustrate that it doesn't matter how little or how much you invest, it's wise to do so no matter the amount. The servant who buries the money in the ground has sinned, though. I don't have much financial knowledge about what makes a sound investment (I recommend any number of financial gurus and websites for advice on that), but my own simple interpretation would be to use your money to help your neighbors in need, to use it wisely in business so that it multiplies, and overall to use it in a way in which you are not attempting to "store up your treasures on earth" and drag it with you to your grave.

In Matthew 6:19–21, it warns us against this attitude toward money, saying:

Do not store up for yourselves treasures on earth, where moths and vermin destroy, and where thieves break in and steal. But store up for yourselves treasures in heaven, where moths and vermin do not destroy, and where thieves do not break in and steal. For where your treasure is, there your heart will be also. (NIV)

Certainly, some fashion purchases are "wise investments" according to the Parable of the Talents. Sometimes, clothing purchases come from a healthy place—of pampering and self-care, which we discussed the importance of in chapter 7; the joy of creating and answering the call of our hearts, which we discussed in chapter 2; or from necessity, like we discussed in chapter 3. At times, a fashion purchase may even be an actual investment that does see a return, like the suit that helps you land the job or the wardrobe upgrade that helps you get a promotion.

As a fashion blogger, I see this principle play out a lot, as buying clothes for me is actually a wise business investment. I can wear one new fifty-dollar item on the blog, and that can potentially yield thousands of dollars (for example) in income from other people buying it via commissions from affiliate links, or from companies who understand this relationship and ask to do sponsorships (they are eager to have some of that magic work on their own brand!).

And yet I've kept the same clothing budget since 2007, way before I started blogging! Buying a lot of fancy clothes or increasing my clothing budget just does not feel like it fits within the limits of my own personal values and beliefs about fashion and faith, nor does it fit with the mission statement of my blog: to normalize budget fashion and emphasize reusing your old clothing. I try to remind myself that I can take that multiplied money and use it in plenty of healthy ways, like giving it to charity, employing more people at my company, or by continuing to multiply it again and again. There's also the basic principle that the more money you spend on clothes, the more "popular" or successful a blog will be. In the fashion world, featuring what's new, exciting, and ultimately expensive is, by and large, the kind of content that will earn you millions of followers.

Despite what could seem like some compelling reasons to spend more on clothing, I'm very conscious of the environment and don't want to waste clothing. (One girl can only wear so many things; there are only so many days in the week!) I can't say that I'm interested in having a popular blog just for the sake of being popular. (The whole point of blogging for me is to achieve my mission statement, not to gain popularity.) And, ultimately, I'd rather save money than spend it! Why buy a new outfit when I can put that money in the bank? This can sometimes put me in the territory of being far too frugal, for sure. (I may be the only woman in America whose husband urges her to go shopping more. It's a running joke in our house.)

You can't and shouldn't want to take your money to the grave with you, I know. And spending on charitable causes, or even invaluable experiences like travel with your spouse or family, can be the best use of money—it's what life's really about. Certainly, it's not healthy to have a fear of poverty, and being super-frugal is not what I recommend. But what about the other end of the money spectrum: That is, when you have a fear of wealth or of having too much money? Let's explore that one next.

The Fear of Wealth

So much of the world's population plays the lottery. The notion of winning is considered a positive experience to the point that we use it as a metaphor for anything good that happens to us ("I feel like I just won the lottery!"). And yet lottery winners often suffer greatly after winning. In his book *Life Lessons from the Lottery: Protecting Your Money in a Scary World*, author Don McNay writes:

> So many [lottery winners] wind up unhappy or wind up broke. People have had terrible things happen . . . People commit suicide. People run through their

money. Easy come, easy go. They go through divorce or people die.[4]

The lottery can actually be quite a dangerous game, akin more to playing Russian roulette. It says in Matthew 19:24: "It is easier for a camel to go through the eye of a needle than for someone who is rich to enter the kingdom of God" (NIV).

In the past I have taken this verse at face value, understanding that being "rich" was the sin itself. Now I see it as a warning that all that money may not be what it's cracked up to be. Why is that?

Money looks really good for so many reasons, but "Mo Money Mo Problems" isn't just a rap song by the Notorious B.I.G.; it's real life. When people come into huge sums of money, it can cause relationship problems. All of a sudden, everyone you know is sucking up and acting like your best friend. Your family members will have strong opinions about how you should spend the money and how much you should give them, because they will expect you to share your winnings. You may decide to buy a new house (why wouldn't you?) and the interior design process is so stressful that it threatens to break up your marriage. It's easy to be blind to the fact that you are literally arguing and stressing over . . . how to spend the money!

Too much money can also desensitize you to luxury experiences and leave you feeling less grateful for them. I don't know about you, but if I won the lottery I'd only want to stay at the Ritz-Carlton maybe once a year. The rest of the time I'd want to stay in less luxurious hotels so my yearly splurge would always feel special. When I was a child, we almost never ate out, and I was in my midtwenties before I experienced an expensive restaurant. I remember how special that experience was. As

---

4   Sam Oh, "Getting Rich Doesn't Have to Change Successful Entrepreneurs for the Worse," *Entrepreneur*, September 30, 2016, https://www.entrepreneur.com/article/281544.

much as I can, I always want to maintain that childlike wonder when it comes to luxuries, and I never want to lose my sense of gratitude, especially for those things that many people are never blessed to have. I want thankfulness and kindness to be so deeply rooted in my soul that I don't take one moment for granted, and I don't ever want to become indifferent—or worse, greedy.

1 Timothy 6:10 warns us: "For the love of money is a root of all kinds of evil. Some people, eager for money, have wandered from the faith and pierced themselves with many griefs" (NIV).

One of my core beliefs is that as humans, we can't always correctly identify what is good and what is bad for us, and the lottery is the perfect example of how something that's almost always labeled as "good" can actually have disastrous effects on our lives. In the same way, things I would normally label as absolutely devastating in my own life—malignant tumors, divorce, losing my job—were painful but also yielded some of the best fruits. Not in spite of them happening, but because they happened. We're all told to look for "the silver lining" or stay positive when bad things happen to us, but I actually believe we should at times rejoice in the "bad" thing itself. When we read the book of Job we see how upbeat and faithful he stays in the face of death, disease, and financial ruin, and in 2 Corinthians 12:10, Paul writes from prison that he actually "delights" in these things! "For Christ's sake, I delight in weaknesses, in insults, in hardships, in persecutions, in difficulties. For when I am weak, then I am strong" (NIV).

I often think about this mislabeling of good and bad when I walk my dog. Bella has zero ability to identify between friend and foe, danger and safety. One time, she developed a sudden and unreasonable fear of a handicapped sign. A sign. It had been in the parking lot for months, but one day she took notice and would cower past it with her tail between her legs. But then we will pass a pleasant dog behind the safety of a fence, and her hair stands up, she starts viciously barking, and she doesn't understand that we are totally safe. Or a car comes barreling down the street, we both nearly escape death, and she is completely oblivious, even wandering at the end of her leash toward the direction of the oncoming car. She is the epitome of us in our humanness—like her, we cannot always correctly identify when something is harmless (like losing a job when something really good is going to happen as a result) or when we are in danger (like when we've won the lottery, which may result in turmoil). I wish she had more faith in the one controlling her leash (for us, that's God), because that would seriously help her anxiety. Also, if you know of any good dog trainers, let me know.

My fear of wealth comes from a mix of the belief that "good" things like winning the lottery are not always good and can potentially be detrimental to relationships, put our salvation in danger (see Mark 10:27), or even change our personality. It also comes from my own personal experience, though—a little taste of "hitting the lottery" in real life. Not exactly the Powerball or the state lottery you're thinking of, but certainly a type of blogging lottery.

Imagine, for a moment, that one day you notice $10,000 in your bank account. (I was making approximately $1,000 per month from freelance writing at the time so, to visualize what this felt like, take whatever monthly income you make now and add a zero—it was a lot!) When this happened to me in August 2012, I thought there had been some mistake. For sure someone was going to ask for that money back. But, after that first deposit, around that same amount or more kept coming, like clockwork, month after month. The commission I was making through affiliate links on my blog had suddenly blown up overnight and stayed at that level month after month, year after year. Four years later, I've generated a million dollars in revenue from blogging, through a number of different monetization methods. Those may not be Powerball numbers, but it's certainly more than this Kansas farm girl ever expected to make.

Being on the receiving end of that kind of money felt like someone hit the reset button on all those great lessons about saving I'd learned growing up. My frugality was replaced with incessant thoughts of, How do I spend this money? I started looking into upgrading my apartment to a house, buying a new car, buying more expensive clothes. Because, in America, we're taught that if our income increases, our spending needs to as well, right?

Rick Warren, pastor and author of The *Purpose Driven Life: What on Earth Am I Here For?*, has made an estimated $100 million from his bestselling books.[5] I can't imagine that Pastor Warren and his wife ever expected to be making that much money. Being a pastor and writing books are not great ways of making money, unless you hit what writer Elizabeth Gilbert calls "freakish success," which Rick Warren did. Faced with this "dilemma" of a new, unimagined income bracket, he and his wife bucked the trend and did something out of the ordinary. They made a commitment to reverse-tithe, or give away 90 percent and keep only 10 percent of what they made.[6] I really respect the Warrens for making that decision, and for sharing that publicly to set an example of thinking about money in a different way.

My own experience was obviously on a much, much smaller scale than the Warrens'. But I can assure you that I was still elated with my good fortune, because bills are real and financial security is an incredible feeling. No one will argue that wondering how you are going to pay your rent or try to move out of your parents' house or get off the streets is glamorous. Money solves palpable problems in many ways. Let's be real. But after that elated first emotion (This is awesome!) came a second, more unexpected friend: sadness and discontent.

---

5   "Rick Warren Net Worth," BornRich (website), accessed June 11, 2017, http://www.bornrich.com/rick-warren.html.

6   Warren Cole Smith and Rusty Leonard, "Book Royalties Allow Some Preachers to Live Like Kings," *The Baptist Messenger*, November 30, 2009, https://www.baptistmessenger.com/book-royalties-allow-some -preachers-to-live-like-kings.

Thinking about spending money all the time makes you really, really sad, and looking around at what others have is a good way to ruin your own life. It took one day of house hunting with a Realtor and suddenly everything in my world looked ugly and gray. I came back to my tiny apartment (the same one that looked huge after my trip to Africa), my same old car, and my same old clothes, and I suddenly wanted more. I had been completely content in my circumstances up till then, and now I suddenly wanted to upgrade everything, all because I had the money in my account. It was totally human nature, and totally preposterous at the same time.

In many ways, it was the fulfillment of Ecclesiastes 5:10: "Whoever loves money never has enough; whoever loves wealth is never satisfied with their income. This too is meaningless" (NIV).

I have never been more thankful for my frugal upbringing, because after one splurge purchase (Invisalign, of all things), I stopped thinking about how to spend the money. It hadn't been a good use of my time, and I certainly was not okay with allowing those thoughts to permeate my current thankfulness for my car, my apartment, or my life. I recognized what was going on—this is what that camel and the needle thing is all about!—and refused to be anything but thankful for everything I already had. Lottery winners are required by law to go on public record when they win, but I kept my earnings to myself. I was single so there were no conversations over how to spend the money. I may have been tempted to upgrade things, but my frugal nature won out, and I decided to keep my lifestyle exactly the same. I happily lived off 10 percent of my company's revenue, while taxes took a big chunk, and of course I continued tithing and giving to charity. The rest I saved for an emergency fund, and I bought a house and paid for our wedding several years later. (And yes, I'm still driving that same old car and wearing many of the same old clothes!)

Having pondered money's wide and varied pitfalls—from shopping too much to not shopping enough, and fearing both wealth and poverty—let's continue on our quest to answer the question we posed at the start of the chapter: How much money should we spend on fashion? We'll start by first exploring what an ideal relationship with money looks like.

Finding the Balance: A Healthy Relationship with Money

In the years leading up to "hitting the blogging lottery," I experienced a very real, very stressful financial situation. In the fall of 2010, I lost my job. By early 2011, unemployment checks had run out, and I couldn't find any work in my industry (marketing/media). I was newly single and on my own for the first time in my life, and I had no idea how I was going to pay my rent. I had gone from having a financial safety net courtesy of my grandfather (he made a good amount of money later in life from the sale of his farm and spoiled me rotten as a child), to the financial safety net of my father (he assumed the role of piggy bank once Grandpa passed), to the financial safety net of my first husband, with hardly any time in between. All of those safety nets were gone, and I found myself totally on my own financially for the first time in my life.

It was a difficult season, but I am so thankful for the biggest lesson I took away from it, which is identifying and understanding where money comes from. God is my Provider, not anyone or anything else on earth, not even a job or an employer. (And, might I add, as a strong female, I never want to feel again that I need a man to provide for me! This is such a healthy place to be, for so many reasons outside of the context of faith.) Many Bible verses identify God as our Provider, from encouraging us not to worry with the promise that our food, shelter, and clothing will be provided (Matthew 6), to relaying the story of fish and loaves and Jesus feeding the masses (in the New Testament). It tells us in 1 Chronicles 29:11–12 that God is the source of all wealth and honor:

Yours, Lord, is the greatness and the power
and the glory and the majesty and the splendor,
for everything in heaven and earth is yours . . .

Wealth and honor come from you;
you are the ruler of all things.

In your hands are strength and power
to exalt and give strength to all. (NIV)

I promised God to never again make the mistake of not giving
Him the credit for providing for me. I will never forget the prayer that
I prayed:

> God, it's just you and me now. I don't know why I
> was so focused on the earthly security that comes
> from money and, specifically, on depending on men
> to provide, for so long, but you are, and always have
> been, my Provider. Even when you provided through
> my earthly father and my husband, YOU were always
> my Provider; it came from you. And no matter how
> you provide for me now—it could be through a job
> or through my blog—I will always, always know and
> understand that money comes from you, and I prom-
> ise to never lose sight of that.

Once we correctly identify the source of our provisions and money,
the next step is having faith and peace of mind that God will always be
faithful in providing for us, and to learn to be content in all situations.
Because while I may ping-pong at times between a fear that I won't have
enough money and a fear of being given too much money, shouldn't my
faith be great enough to trust God through both? Through any and all

situations with money, whether things are tight, or when great wealth challenges us spiritually, we can pray earnestly from Philippians 4:11–13:

> For I have learned to be content, whatever the circum-stances. I know what it is to be in need, and I know what it is to have plenty. I have learned the secret of being content in any and every situation, whether well fed or hungry, whether living in plenty or in want. I can do all this through him who gives me strength. (NIV)

Of course, having total faith can be easier said than done, and hindsight is often 20/20. During one financially strapped time right after college, I sold my car, packed up a few belongings, and moved to Boston without a place to live or a permanent job. For several months, I took odd jobs through a temp agency and didn't make even remotely enough to pay my rent. I lived off ten-cent frozen burritos, walked the long two miles to the grocery store, and didn't indulge in anything extra. It was a time of great faith, because I knew I would find a job eventually, but it was also an incredibly anxiety-ridden time. And sure, it's easy for me to view losing my job in 2010 as a blessing today, because now I know that as a result of that hardship my blog was born, but it can be (understandably) easy to give in to a fear of poverty in those seasons, and praying from Philippians 4:6–7 can help. I love the sooth-ing description of peace that "surpasses all understanding," don't you?

> Do not be anxious about anything, but in every situ-ation, by prayer and petition, with thanksgiving, present your requests to God. And the peace of God, which transcends all understanding, will guard your hearts and minds through Christ Jesus. (NIV)

We can strive to be content in all things, and in all financial situations, and when money does come we can use Scriptures for plenty of advice on what to do with it—the very first step being tithing, which is encouraged in Proverbs 3:9–10 and other verses to give joyfully the "firstfruits" of our crops:

> Honor the Lord with your wealth,
> with the firstfruits of all your crops;
> then your barns will be filled to overflowing,
> and your vats will brim over with new wine. (NIV)

Tithing to your church is one way to give, and charity and helping our neighbors with their immediate needs is another. When I start to feel pressure about finances, or like I'm not readily giving with a cheerful spirit, I like to sit in prayer with my hands physically open, and manifest in my heart the willingness to give, give, give. As it says in Matthew 25:35–36, 40 giving to others is a cornerstone to the call of our lives and the meaning of life:

> For I was hungry and you gave me something to eat, I
> was thirsty and you gave me something to drink, I was
> a stranger and you invited me in, I needed clothes and
> you clothed me, I was sick and you looked after me,
> I was in prison and you came to visit me. . . . 'Truly I
> tell you, whatever you did for one of the least of these
> brothers and sisters of mine, you did for me. (NIV)

Interestingly, the idea of keeping your hands open may start as a focus on giving to others and releasing your wealth, but in keeping your hands open, you are also performing the same action that allows you to receive. A clinched fist unwilling to give is also unable to receive. This openhanded concept plays out in the Parable of the Talents that we discussed earlier, which encourages us not to hoard money in a tight fist, but to let it go and use it to make wise investments, so that it multiples, earning us the praise of "well done good and faithful servant."

Beyond being open to giving with a cheerful heart, we also find in Scripture plenty of commandments to keep our priorities straight, to pursue God and not wealth, and to shift our focus from believing in, striving for, and seeking money to believing in, striving for, and seeking God. In Luke 16:13, it says: "No one can serve two masters. Either you will hate the one and love the other, or you will be devoted to the one and despise the other. You cannot serve both God and money" (NIV).

1 Timothy 6:10–11 echoes the same sentiment:

> For the love of money is a root of all kinds of evil. Some people, eager for money, have wandered from the faith and pierced themselves through with many griefs. But you, man of God, flee from all this, and pursue righteousness, godliness, faith, love, endurance and gentleness. (NIV)

To honor these commands, I find it helpful to continuously check in with myself about whether I'm developing any emotional connection to money, shopping, and clothes. In chapter 2, I mentioned that my closet could burn down and I wouldn't shed a tear. I'm attracted to the process of being creative with clothes—a process that is spiritual for me and answers the call of my heart—but not to the things themselves. It's important for me to keep in mind that my closet and the physical things there have no real meaning to life or power over me.

This outlook is outlined in 1 Timothy 6:17–19:

> Command those who are rich in this present world not to be arrogant nor to put their hope in wealth, which is so uncertain, but to put hope in God, who

richly provides us with everything for our enjoyment. Command them to do good, to be rich in good deeds, and to be generous and willing to share. In this way they will lay up treasure for themselves as a firm foundation for the coming age, so that they may take hold of the life that is truly life. (NIV)

Scripture is a constant source of spiritual guidance when it comes to navigating the sometimes powerful hold that money and finances can have on our lives. But if we are to follow Scripture in our everyday lives, we must ask, what is the *practical* application of these Scriptures when it comes to money? What does a healthy relationship with finances and a passion for clothing, hair, makeup, or any of the arts look like? Let's get real in the next section and talk about setting and sticking to a clothing budget.

How to Set a Clothing Budget

In my early twenties I was too frugal to buy a suit I needed for a job interview, and now ten years later I indulge in (almost) guilt-free clothing shopping on a regular basis. What happened that got me from point A to point B? The huge turning point for me was setting a clothing budget.

It was my practical application of all the money advice I had gleaned from the Bible. It took the emotion out of money for me and created a sense of peace, knowing that the money I was spending was predetermined, or earmarked, to be spent on clothes.

I'll admit that the word "budget" can be a total bore. I'm not a math person, and I don't like having limits on what I can spend, even if they are self-imposed—I'm already so frugal, it seemed excessive at first to monitor myself further! But setting a clothing budget actually set me free. Before I set a budget, I could picture myself shackled in chains—bound to a fear of poverty, fear of not being a good steward of money, or fear of caring about clothes too much. Setting a budget that honored my faith and personal values was the key that would unlock those chains for me, giving me the freedom to express myself through clothing.

Having money set aside for clothing for the first time in my life felt a lot like breaking out of self-imposed jail. I made a deal with myself— I was not allowed to feel guilty when I stayed within that budget. I had already given myself the go-ahead, and what I spent within those limits was no one's business (take that, fashion guilt!). It didn't happen overnight, but the guilt started to subside as I embraced this newfound freedom.

But the freedom I felt was just the start. Take, for example, these additional compelling benefits and reasons for setting a clothing budget:

Clothing budgets reduce stress. When you commit yourself in advance to a realistic amount you can afford within your budget, you no longer have to worry about any particular purchase. The fear or apprehension you previously felt when buying clothes goes away, and the experience becomes entirely stress-free.

Clothing budgets relieve guilt. All that buyer's guilt goes away. If you normally feel remorseful after purchases, or experience mom guilt when you spend money on yourself, having a budget will help relieve that uncomfortable feeling.

Clothing budgets create family peace. If you're married or sharing your finances with someone, having a set budget can be a great way to bring peace to your home. You don't need to discuss purchases with your spouse or partner, and you don't need to hide your shopping bags. If it's in the budget that you mutually agreed upon, then it's fair game.

Clothing budgets help with purchasing decisions. When you have a clothing budget, it can be helpful to imagine purchases as slices of a pie. How many slices is this purchase going to take? If it's half my pie for the month, then it may not be worth it, even if it's on sale. A huge part of loving your personal style is being a smart shopper, and having a budget can greatly help in this area.

Once you've committed to a clothing budget, you'll probably find yourself saying, "If only I'd known how awesome this would be, I would've done it so much sooner!" So how do you actually go about setting one? I'm so glad you asked, because we are going to run through how to do that next.

When I set my budget in 2007, I needed things in pretty much every category. I was living in cold, snowy Boston—so my list included things like boots, coats, suits for work, and casual clothes. I settled on $250 per month. Even today, that still feels like a lot of money, but it was reasonable within the big picture at the time. It was on the higher end of the percentage of take-home income that financial planners recommend (usually 2 to 8 percent), but I was completely debt-free: I had ditched the exorbitant Boston rent in favor of a very affordable, "charming" new place with a missing dining room window that I shared with two women from my church, and I didn't own a car. I hardly ever spent money on, well, anything. So that $250 was my "fun money" as much as it was money for clothing necessities.

These are the guiding principles I used to set my budget. They can you get started if you're thinking about setting a clothing budget of your own!

Your income. Most financial planners recommend setting aside 2 to 8 percent of your take-home income for clothing.[7] Which is a great starting point but can actually be a pretty large range. So keep reading for more factors to consider.

Your family. Consider how many people are included in your budget. Do you have children or a spouse, or is this budget just for one person?

Your job. If you're a lawyer, then higher-quality business-like outfits can actually impact your success. If you're a nurse who wears scrubs, though, you can save a considerable amount on clothing since you only need clothes for weekends and social occasions.

Your expenses. Take note of how much are you spending on other essential categories, like housing and living expenses, to determine how much room you comfortably have to spend on clothing.

Your financial goals. Consider whether you are saving money for a house or paying off debt. If you have significant financial goals or stressors, then you'll want to reduce your clothing budget as much as possible to make room for these other (more important) categories. I don't recommend completely doing away with your clothing budget

7   "10 Recommended Category Percentages for Your Family Budget," *Leave Debt Behind* (blog), accessed June 11, 2017, http://www.leavedebtbehind .com/frugal-living/budgeting/10-recommended-category-percentages-for -your-family-budget.

if at all possible, though—because if you close off the category entirely, that can actually hurt more than help by leading to sporadic, unplanned spending.

Your hobbies. If you care more about travel or building a music library more than clothing, you may want to reduce your clothing budget to the lower end of the income percentage and move the excess funds into other categories that interest you more.

Your values. Consider your tithing commitment, as well as charitable giving, disaster relief, and/or helping a neighbor in need. You may opt to spend more in these types of categories that mean the most to you.

Your shopping habits. Do you tend to shop often, or only a couple of times a year? If you shop often, consider setting a monthly clothing budget. If you only shop one or two times a year, or for big life events like a pregnancy or a new job, then a clothing budget can be for just one shopping trip or the entire year.

When you establish a clothing budget, you've done most of the work upfront. Once the budget is set, you shouldn't have to think about it again, unless your financial situation changes. The only real "maintenance" is ensuring that you stick to your budget, so here are a few tips for that:

Define the category. What you include in your clothing budget is totally up to you, but it's good to have clear boundaries at the outset. Will your clothing budget include things like alterations, dry cleaning, undergarments, and shipping charges?

Keep track. If you don't write down your purchases, it can seem like you're spending way more than you actually are, or vice versa. The best way to keep yourself honest is by simply writing everything down as you go. No need to get fancy: a simple memo app on your phone or a notepad and pen will do.

Carry over. With a monthly clothing budget, you could implement a "use it or lose it" strategy, but that can encourage buying something you don't really need just to use up that month's allotment. Carrying over to the next month allows you to save up for a luxury item, or you save some of your budget for the best times of year to score great deals, like right after Christmas and in late June / early July (when the clothing seasons change).

Return or deduct your overages. Sometimes our eyes are bigger than our wallets. No biggie. Whenever this happens to me, I go through my purchases that month and pick a few things to return. If I really like everything, then I take the items out of next month's budget, or I simply go back and buy them next month.

For the Rebecca Bloomwoods of the world, having a clothing budget can help curb overspending and the sometimes damaging quest for that next great purchase. It can also help curb underspending and encourage us to invest in quality clothing that is more appropriate for our jobs and lifestyles. Maybe you're in a season when it's time to pull back from spending so much on clothes. Or maybe you're in a season when God is encouraging you to invest time and money into your wardrobe, for any number of reasons. A clothing budget ultimately helps with both.

I hope the biggest thing you take away from this chapter, though, is an understanding that just because it's possible to get into trouble with clothes—whether it's through overspending or overzealous frugality—shopping itself isn't inherently bad. Having a healthy relationship with money and clothing is absolutely possible within the context of our faith and personal values. It's a lifelong journey, of course, and not something you should expect to have figured out overnight. I hope sharing my struggles with money in this chapter has encouraged you in your own journey. With a little prayer and self-guidance, there's no reason to feel guilty about enjoying personal style, especially when there are so many ways to do it responsibly—both from a financial and global perspective. Which brings us to our next topic: Buying clothes on a budget is one thing, but how can we also be environmentally and socially responsible fashion consumers with our clothing purchases?

Chapter 9

How Can I Be a Responsible Fashion Consumer?

For as long as I can remember, my clothing mantra has been "budget, budget, budget" and "cheap, cheap, cheap." As a physical metaphor, my blog would be a mob picketing with signs that say things like "fashion is not just for the rich and famous" or "you don't need a million bucks to look like a million bucks." Since I first started blogging in 2010, I have been standing up for myself and women everywhere by advocating that we shouldn't be excluded from enjoying nice things no matter the size of our budgets.

Knowing my personal story, of where and how I grew up, and how much frugality was the focus in our home, it's not hard to see why I landed on this mantra. When I first learned about the concept of blogging, I thought, *Finally! Now we can talk about real stuff that real people wear—affordable fashion!* (what I deemed "everyday fashion"). I loved reading fashion magazines, but I also felt incredibly left out. I never believed I could look great, because I thought I would never have enough money or want to spend $10,000 on one outfit. I wanted to feel included in fashion and to invite other women to feel included right alongside me.

Keep in mind that back when I started blogging, the terms "Maxxinista" and "fashion on a budget" were not a part of our everyday lingo yet. Designer collaborations at Target were just starting to become a regular thing. By recreating celebrity outfits for a lot less, and rebelliously doing side-by-side comparisons with my picture beside theirs, I set out to prove that you don't need tons of money to dress that way. I was preaching to myself as a little girl who never would've believed being stylish on a budget was possible. And, my biggest hope: I wanted to inspire others to feel the same way, and to not feel rejected or left out of the fashion industry like I had!

Seven years later, we see massive amounts of this kind of messaging. "Look for less" is everywhere we turn, and budget fashion has never been more sought after. In some ways I believe budget fashion will always be second tier and luxury fashion will always reign supreme, but it's also a much different landscape now. There's simply not as much shame in saving money. At a bargain clothing store today you'll find members of every economic status, side-by-side, shopping together. How little you paid for something is the new bragging right. Even celebrities are onboard, mixing "high and low," opting to wear a luxury piece with something budget-friendly, and budget items are often featured alongside more expensive pieces in magazines. Saving money has become cool in its own right.

Thanks to this (wonderful) transformation in fashion journalism and the industry overall, my constant "cheap, cheap, cheap" mantra isn't as needed now, and certainly not as loudly. Because there's less of a need, I find myself loosening my grip on the mantra of cheap clothing and shifting my mission statement. Beyond the larger landscape becoming more inclusive of budget fashion, there are other experiences that have also been hugely influential in changing my outlook and focus.

For example, I used to be the sort of shopper who would only buy things if they were ten dollars. I wasn't that concerned with how much I liked an item, and I wasn't concerned with how well it fit, I just wanted the absolute best deal. It was the challenge for me with fashion—I didn't care if I had the best outfit in the room, I wasn't going for best dressed. I wanted to be the woman whose outfit cost the least. I only shopped the markdown clearance section and prided myself on having the cheapest clothes.

But as I entered my thirties, that changed. I naturally started wanting higher-quality items. I'd learned my lesson from buying inexpensive pieces that, after one wash, would look terrible or fall apart. And I realized that I'd been buying things that I didn't even want to wear! Sure, a shirt might have been ten dollars, but then it would hang in my closet because it was ugly, uncomfortable, or didn't fit. Or I would find myself embarrassed while wearing it. Like that Teletubbies T-shirt I was wearing when I ran into my ex and his new girlfriend. I was wearing it simply because it was free, and that really didn't work out so well, did it? (Spoiler alert: no, no it didn't.) Those experiences and a pile of unworn clothing set off alarm bells in the "wasteful" part of my brain, which started bossing around the "budget" part of my brain, telling it to stop being so cheap and spend a little more so that I could buy things I'd actually wear and keep forever. A ten-dollar shirt is actually quite expensive if you never take it off the hanger, and I hate wasting things more than I hate spending money.

Beyond sheer practicality, my fashion point of view was also changing because I was making more money, as many people do as they advance in their career. I started to crave things that were of a higher quality, would last longer, and that I knew would never go out of style. When I splurged on a careful, thoughtful style choice, like my $257 black leather jacket in 2012, I noticed that I wore it constantly, year after year. I became interested in making more of those types of purchases. There's a natural progression that happens inside of many women's closets when they hit their thirties, as it certainly did for me. Instead of $10 to $20 being the maximum amount I'd pay for a shirt, I found myself willing to pay $30, $40, or even $60 in some cases, and postpurchase, I felt great. I liked the $60 shirt so much more, and wore it so many more times, that it felt completely worth it to me. I didn't increase my budget: I was just willing to buy fewer items but spend more on each one than I ever had in the past.

Perhaps the biggest factor that's quieted my old "cheap, cheap, cheap" mantra, though, has been a recent awakening to the issues raised by the ethical fashion movement. Akin to the food movement, where buying organic foods and eating at farm-to-table restaurants is becoming more and more popular, the ethical fashion movement has dramatically changed what we know about how our clothing is made. The media is starting to cover the hidden dilemmas of the clothing industry, and documentaries like *The True Cost* are making their way into popular culture. The ways in which the people making our clothing are being mistreated and the devastating effects the garment industry is having on the environment are trickling into the consciousness of the larger population.

I have been reached by those little trickles through random news stories, articles posted in my social feed, and recommendations from readers. I've also had several serendipitous experiences and met friends who I feel were put into my path for very good reason. Thanks to those experiences and influences, I am starting to wake up to these important fashion issues; I'm becoming more and more concerned for the environment and fair wages in regards to my clothing purchases.

This awakening has not been easy for me. In fact, I'd describe it as mostly painful. I already have loads of things to feel guilty about when it comes to fashion, thanks to my faith and personal values. When I see messaging about being a responsible consumer, it's tempting to shut down. I already feel like every fashion decision I make is so calculated, so careful, so meticulously mapped out that I simply can't imagine factoring in other concerns. But in what I now consider the trifecta of being an ethical clothing consumer, I was missing one of the three categories completely. I had the faith thing down, I had the personal values down, but I was totally and completely overlooking social consciousness and honoring my global responsibility.

As I've become more aware of this new (to me) concern and this new way of being an ethical consumer, I am faced with so many questions: What exactly does it mean to be globally responsible with fashion? How many clothes should we feel okay about owning? And, ultimately, how can we be responsible fashion consumers?

The Precious Human Lives Behind Our Clothes

As soon as news broke of the earthquakes in Haiti in 2010, Julie boarded a plane. She didn't know how she would help, but she was determined to make a difference. Living in a tent near the Port-au-Prince airport during the relief effort, she developed a plan to help Haiti rebuild. She noticed abandoned tires in abundance on the side of the road and that what people needed most were jobs. So she concocted a plan to mix the two—an overabundance and a need—by employing people to make sandals out of old tires. They called it Deux Mains, or "two hands" in French. It symbolizes what two hands can do, both the Haitians' hands that create beautiful sandals and accessories, and the hands of the customers who, through their purchases, make a difference.

My husband, Joshua, grew up in Haiti and was connected with Julie in the infancy of her company. Over the years, he became a board member and one of her trusted advisors. I knew Julie socially, but Deux Mains and their mission were not at the forefront of my world until the summer of 2015. My husband asked me to accompany him on a board trip to Haiti. In my head, I was going on vacation, to see my husband's childhood home and the country he loves so much, but it turned out to be much, much more than that.

During our trip, I tagged along to board meetings, I went on a tour of the Deux Mains workshop and boutique, and I met all of the artisans who work there. During one lunch, the artisans shared their stories with us through a translator. One of Deux Mains's first employees, Jolina, told her story. She said: "After the earthquake, Julie could've brought me rice and beans, but that would be gone by now. Instead, she gave me a job and gave me my life back."

Effectively helping countries like Haiti is an incredibly complex topic that I don't understand fully (our discussion in chapter 7 just barely skimmed the surface!), but I do know that because of Deux Mains's fair-wages policy, each of the twenty-one employees supports an average of eight to ten people with their paycheck (as the employees told me). Creating jobs in Haiti is the difference between charity and changing things from the inside out. There is, of course, still much work to do: Haiti's unemployment rate was 40.6 percent in 2010, with more than two-thirds of the labor force unable to find formal jobs, and their economic struggle continues today.[1]

The trip to Haiti turned out to not be the vacation I was expecting but an experience that would have a big impact on me both personally and professionally. Given everything I saw, I really wanted to do something to help. The Deux Mains workshop had recently upped their productivity, but as a result they had a stockpile of inventory and needed sales to move that inventory. I pitched to Julie and the board the idea of doing a flash sale on my blog, and they said yes. We put together the details, and it was live before I was back in the States. The week of the flash sale, Deux Mains sold more through their website than they ever had in the lifetime of the company (up to that point, they'd focused mainly on wholesale selling). The sale cleared the stockpiled inventory and gave the company a huge boost. It will forever be one of my favorite accomplishments with J's Everyday Fashion!

Prior to my experience with Deux Mains, I'd had some exposure to the ethical fashion movement. A friend I met early on in my blogging

---

1 *The World Factbook,* "Central America and Caribbean: Haiti," Central Intelligence Agency, accessed June 11, 2017, https://www.cia.gov/library /publications/the-world-factbook/geos/ha.html.

career, Katie Martinez, has a company called Elegantees. Based in New York City, they employ women in Nepal who are survivors of sex trafficking and provide them with fair wages. I partnered with Katie off and on for many years on my blog, dating back to 2010, and I have always admired my sweet friend and her business. But it wasn't until I actually saw an ethical fashion company in action in Haiti that all the dots fully connected for me. I started to wonder, *Who made my clothes? Were those workers treated ethically?* It was suddenly clear how important ethical fashion is. It's a basic human right and not just feel-good thrills or a passing trend.

For many consumers, the wake-up call to ethical fashion occurred in 2013, when an eight-story building known as Rana Plaza in Bangladesh collapsed. More than 1,100 people lost their lives and 2,500 more were injured.[2] Cracks had appeared in the structure in the days and weeks before, and building owners were warned it could collapse. And yet garment workers were ordered to return to work anyway because the profits were too important to pass up. It was the deadliest accidental structure failure in modern history. According to press accounts, major brands like Benetton, the Children's Place, Joe Fresh, Monsoon Accessorize, Mango, Primark, and Walmart had manufactured goods in that building.[3] How much responsibility, exactly, do these brands have to make sure that the overseas workers who produce their goods are being taken care of and treated fairly?

When one of the Deux Mains artisans was hit by a bus last year, Julie continued to pay that worker's wages even though she was unable to work, and she got her job back as soon as she recovered. That was

---

2   Sarah Butler, "Bangladeshi Factory Deaths Spark Action Among High-Street Clothing Chains," *Guardian* (Manchester), June 22, 2013, https://www.theguardian.com/world/2013/jun/23/rana-plaza-factory-disaster-bangladesh-primark.

3   "2013 Savar Building Collapse," Wikipedia, accessed June 11, 2017, https://en.wikipedia.org/wiki/2013_Savar_building_collapse.

going way above and beyond because labor laws and insurance largely don't exist in many garment-producing countries, and even if they do, they are often not honored. If a worker is injured, even because of their job, they will not be paid while they recover, and they will not have a job waiting for them once they are healthy. The women and children who lost their husbands and fathers in the building collapse at Rana Plaza didn't have insurance and are now desolate with no way to support themselves or make money. (That's what makes ethical fashion companies like Deux Mains different—they treat their workers well, even if local laws don't require them to.)

We might view the conditions in Rana Plaza and other countries as solely an international manufacturing issue, but it's not. Certainly, we produce far less clothing here in the United States than we ever have. As recently as the 1960s, 95 percent of the clothing American companies manufactured was made in US factories; today American garment manufacturers produce only about 2 percent domestically, while the other 98 percent is outsourced to developing countries around the world. But if you think you can avoid contributing to the problem by always buying American, think again. In 2012 the U.S. Department of Labor did a sweep of garment factories in Los Angeles's Fashion District and found widespread "sweatshop-like" labor violations, including paying workers far less than the minimum wage, not paying them overtime, and falsifying or failing to maintain records.[4] It appears to be much more of a clothing-industry problem than an international problem.

While situations like the Rana Plaza collapse have put pressure on companies to maintain healthy working conditions, progress has been slow. And American consumers are still largely unaware of the

---

4   "Extensive Violations of Federal, State Laws Found Among Garment Contractors at Los Angeles Fashion District Location," news release, United States Department of Labor, December 13, 2012, https://www .dol.gov/opa/media/press/whd/WHD20122378.htm.

issue. One step in the right direction is the California Transparency in Supply Chains Act, which went into effect in 2012 and requires companies based in California with more than $100 million in revenue to make information about their supply chain available to the public.[5] The affected companies must detail their programs and efforts to source products responsibly and show that they are not contributing to human trafficking and slavery.

The California Transparency in Supply Chains Act aims to give consumers the opportunity to make purchasing decisions based on which companies are engaged in ethical manufacturing. It's akin to the Federal Drug Administration requiring nutrition labels. Before the FDA required this, beginning in 1966, there was no way to know what ingredients were in the food you were buying.[6] Today, it's tough to imagine nutritional labels *not* being on food, and yet the garment industry seems to be lagging a good forty years behind, with no required information from companies about their manufacturing practices other than to include tags with "made in [insert country here]." And while about 3,200 California-based companies are now required to provide information,[7] it seems to me that most people don't know that this information exists or where to find it.

For example, one company affected by the California Transparency in Supply Chains Act is J.Crew. Although I'm very familiar with this brand and often shop there, I was unaware until very recently that they

5   "California Transparency in Supply Chains Act," United States Department of Labor, accessed June 11, 2017, https://www.dol.gov/ilab /child-forced-labor/California-Transparency-in-Supply-Chains-Act.htm.
6   "Significant Dates in U.S. Food and Drug Law History," U.S. Food and Drug Administration, accessed June 11, 2017, http://www.fda.gov /AboutFDA/WhatWeDo/History/Milestones/ucm128305.htm.
7   "California Transparency in Supply Chains Act," United States Department of Labor, accessed June 11, 2017, https://www.dol.gov/ilab /child-forced-labor/California-Transparency-in-Supply-Chains-Act.htm.

were governed by this legislation,[8] and that they have disclosure information listed on their websites. They also have two full-time employees dedicated to social responsibility (again, who knew?), and online they list in detail their efforts to audit, monitor, and improve manufacturing conditions for the factories they employ. Here's the issue, though: what exactly do all these big words in their disclosure mean? And when you read through the lengthy document, some red flags pop up. Like this section where they openly admit that they can't catch everything:

> [Like any retailer] our supply chain is complex and we have less visibility of the indirect suppliers who provide fabric, trim and other components to our direct suppliers, and even less visibility of the origin of the raw materials of these components.[9]

In other words—we can communicate with the people who sew the clothes, but those factories may get their zippers, buttons, and fabrics from their own sources (a.k.a. from who knows where), and those people making the buttons or the material that goes into the trim might be slaves, but it would be really hard for us to monitor that. The method that they use to monitor and inspect also has issues:

> A typical inspection consists of document reviews, private worker interviews and a walk-through of the facility. When appropriate, we will also conduct surveillance and off-site interviews.[10]

---

8   Ibid.
9   Ibid.
10   Ibid.

In other words: We visit the factory. They know we are coming so they hide all the child workers. We do interviews, in which the workers feel pressured to tell us that they are being paid fairly or they will lose their jobs. I'm playing devil's advocate here, because what a hot mess, right? From J.Crew's perspective, they are searching for evidence that things are okay, not that things are askew. They don't want to have to find a new factory. Sourcing a factory that makes clothing to standard and for the price consumers want is a huge undertaking, and they are not going to be quick to fire anyone, as you can read in their policy:

> We terminate a business relationship only as a last resort, if a critical issue of noncompliance is identified or when suppliers are unwilling to comply with our requirements despite our efforts to help them become compliant.[11]

And yet, out of all the clothing options I have, I'm more likely to shop J.Crew these days, because at least they are trying, right? They hired two full-time employees to monitor working conditions. And they are disclosing this type of information on their website, even if they are technically required to do so by law. It's a step in the right direction, albeit a baby step.

In the summer of 2016 I was given the opportunity to travel to India so that I could shadow a fair-trade jewelry company called Bajalia on a buying trip. I was excited to learn more about these issues, and see how things are made, and the process clothing and accessories go through to get from conception to our closets.

When we visited the factories and homes where Bajalia goods are made, in a small village several hours outside of New Delhi called Sarai Tarin, we got to see the working conditions up close and speak directly

---

11   Ibid.

to the factory owner who employs the workers. The factory was fair-trade certified to the highest degree. It looked like a lovely place to work and is run by what appears to be a very kind, honest man. A few doors down, we also visited artisans who work in their homes. They were so eager to joyfully make things for us that if I ever get into the business of making products, I would hire them on the spot.

While in New Delhi, we also attended several garment expos held at huge, air-conditioned convention centers. The displays at these shows, I would learn, are handled by middlemen. We asked them if they made the items they were selling themselves, and they hadn't; they were either employed by the manufacturers as representatives or they employ the people who made the goods in factories or homes. The conversation with one of these middlemen would go something like this:

"Are you fair-trade certified? And if not, would you be willing to get certification before we buy from you?"

"Not yet, but we are working on it."

"Are you willing to agree to random audits of your factories and workers?"

"Yes, that would be fine."

A huge national campaign in India right now is "Make in India." (Yes, "Make.") Its purpose is to encourage brands in Europe, America, and Australia to outsource their production to India, and buy their goods from India. While it was much more satisfying to witness the making of goods up close in the villages, at the garment shows it was more of a leap of faith, because it seemed everyone was trying to win our business. It stands to reason that sometimes manufacturers are willing to do whatever it takes to make an American company happy so they can win and keep that business. Ultimately, we've got to work on how and what we demand from suppliers if we want to see effective worldwide change.

Because currently, American brands want the best prices from factories so that they can compete with other American brands. Which is due to American consumers (like me) demanding "cheap, cheap, cheap" and wanting to pay less and less. When you look at the price of clothing over the past twenty years, you should see inflation, but you don't. Things just keep getting cheaper and cheaper. And instead of four seasons in fashion, we now have more like fifty-two seasons a year, with new items arriving in stores every single week, or every single day. The factories are under great pressure for higher output and lower and lower prices, causing them to squeeze workers harder and harder and take advantage of human lives to get the prices and output they need. (They are also using cheap, environmentally harmful fabrics to cut costs, which we'll discuss in the next section.) It's a nasty cycle.

A firsthand story from the documentary The *True Cost* illustrates how workers are sometimes mistreated. A garment worker in Bangladesh named Shima tells the story of how she formed a union with some of her fellow employees because her salary was only ten dollars per month, which was not enough to cover her basic needs. They presented a list of demands to their managers. Of the result, she says:

> [The] managers closed the door. And along with them, 30–40 employees attacked us and they beat us. They used chairs, sticks, scales, and things like scissors to beat [us]. Especially they kicked and punched and they beat [our] heads against the walls. They beat us especially [in the] chest and abdomen.[12]

In 2014, garment workers went on strike in Phnom Penh, Cambodia, to request fair treatment and a living wage. Their resistance and demands were met with physical force. At least four protesters died

---

12 "*The True Cost* Movie Script," Springfield! Springfield!, accessed June 11, 2017, http://www.springfieldspringfield.co.uk/movie_script.php?movie=the-true-cost.

and forty were injured by police brutality in response to their peaceful protests.[13]

Fair wages and working conditions is an ethics issue, no matter what religion you may follow. But certainly, as Christians, we have a responsibility to make a difference in the garment industry; to demand more information about our clothes so that we can make a positive impact with our purchasing decisions.

In Deuteronomy 24:14–15, it says:

> Do not take advantage of a hired worker who is poor and needy, whether that worker is a fellow Israelite or a foreigner residing in one of your towns. Pay them their wages each day before sunset, because they are poor and are counting on it. Otherwise they may cry to the Lord against you, and you will be guilty of sin. (NIV)

In the documentary *Make it in America: Empowering Global Fashion*, Elan Savir, owner of apparel company Elan International, says:

> I believe that the people who make the garment need also need to be happy. I believe that if you bought a shirt and it's being made by people who are suffering and miserable in some far away country, that somehow you will feel that when you're wearing the shirt, I believe that.[14]

---

13 Heng, Sinith, "Violence Erupts in Cambodia as Labor Dispute Intensifies; Four Dead," *CBS News*, January 3, 2014, http://www.cbsnews.com/news/violence-erupts-in-cambodia-as-labor-dispute-intensifies.

14 *Make It in America: Empowering Global Fashion*, Make It in America (website), accessed June 11, 2017, http://www.makeitinamerica.tv.

Before we explore some ways that as consumers we can make a difference with our purchases, let's look at another troubling global issue: the environment and the impact our clothing habits and purchasing patterns have on the planet.

The Precious Planet and Our Clothes

Recently in the news, I saw a story about a girl who reduced her annual waste to the size of half a Mason jar. That's right—all the trash she produced for two years fit into one tiny little jar.[15] I was supremely jealous, because when I was growing up, the message "never waste anything" was right up there with "don't spend money." Don't waste food, don't waste energy (lights) or water, don't waste clothing—save, save, save and always reuse.

Being frugal and not being wasteful often go hand in hand. We see this on the show *Extreme Cheapskates* on TLC, for example. It profiles people in American suburbs who do extreme things to save money—like peeing in a jar instead of using the toilet, diving into dumpsters for food and household items, and making their own toothpaste, dental floss, and reusable toilet paper. They obsess over not wasting anything in order to save a buck.

While I may not go as far as the people featured on the show, I'm still extremely frugal. On my blog I have always challenged myself to reuse clothing I already own, wearing the same items over and over again, and styling the items in new and different ways. First and foremost, this is a great money-saving tactic; it's cheaper to use what's already in your closet than to go to the mall.

---

15   "This Woman Can Fit Two Years of Trash in One Small Mason Jar,"
      Inhabitat (website), June 18, 2016, http://inhabitat.com/this-woman
      -can-fit-two-years-of-trash-in-one-small-mason-jar.

Waste affects much more than just our pocketbooks, though. According to the Environmental Protection Agency, each year Americans throw away 12.7 million tons of textiles, or sixty-eight pounds per person.[16] That number includes things like sheets and towels, but still—sixty-eight pounds?! Per person?! Clothing is approximately 5 percent of our landfill waste,[17] and clothing is the second most wasteful industry after oil, thanks to the pesticides used to grow cotton, dyes used to color clothing, water consumed in the process of making clothing, and the eventual landfill waste produced when clothing is discarded.[18]

In other countries I've visited, the trash is everywhere—in piles on the street, clogging rivers and waterways. There are no formal trash systems, and people just throw it on the ground. Sometimes I use those experiences to convince myself that we have a great system here in America. We put our trash neatly into little bags. Trash collectors come and pick it up and pack it away. And from there, we never see it again! It really is quite a tidy, convenient system for handling our trash. That is, until we come in contact with a landfill.

Every time I see video footage of a landfill or drive by one, I get this strange prickly sensation all over my body. Even from a very young age, it just all seemed so *wrong*. Like, why aren't the adults doing something about this? I don't claim to know much about science or utility companies or the best way to handle trash—that's definitely not the

---

16 Luz Claudio, "Waste Couture: Environmental Impact of the Clothing Industry," *Environmental Health Perspectives* 115, no. 9 (September 2007): A449–A454, https://www.ncbi.nlm.nih.gov/pmc/articles /PMC3018514/?report=classic.

17 Council for Textile Recycling (website), June 11, 2017, http://www .weardonaterecycle.org.

18 Glynis Sweeny, "Fast Fashion Is the Second Dirtiest Industry in the World, Next to Big Oil," EcoWatch, August 17, 2015, http://www .ecowatch.com/fast-fashion-is-the-second-dirtiest-industry-in-the -world-next-to-big--1882083445.html.

way my brain works. But the way we do things now doesn't necessarily seem right, either.

Because even though our neat little bags go away and we never see them again, we certainly don't have our act together when it comes to trash in America. Maybe we're better at putting it out of sight, but we also are going through enormous amounts of stuff at what feels like an alarmingly fast rate. I mean, sixty-eight pounds of textiles per person each year just doesn't seem right, does it? I really want to believe that I've never thrown away that many clothes in my life, let alone in one year. When towels become threadbare, they become towels for the dog. When a shirt gets holes in it, it becomes a rag. I try to only buy things that I will wear and wear, and keep for life. I have a fairly impressive collection of clothing from eight to ten years ago (when I first started shopping) that I still wear. But that still may not be enough.

Two "science experiments" in the documentary *Slowing Down Fast Fashion* really brought these environmental issues to light for me. In one scene, host Alex James places two black crewneck sweaters side by side. One is made of wool, and the other is made of acrylic. They are impossible to tell apart; they look and feel so much alike. But when James sets fire to them, the difference becomes sickeningly clear. The acrylic sweater combusts and turns into a pile of goo within minutes. It's reduced to what looks like oil and smells strongly of chemicals, because acrylic is essentially plastic. But the wool sweater won't catch on fire at all. The blowtorch burns a hole in it, but the natural fibers immediately extinguish themselves.

In the second experiment, two similar sweaters are buried underground for four months. When James digs up the wool sweater, it's almost halfway gone, it has biodegraded so quickly. The acrylic sweater, though, looks just like new—it hasn't started to biodegrade at all. Companies use acrylic because it's cheaper. And cheaper is what we asked for. ("We" meaning me!) But when we buy cheap, we're creating waste that's going to be on this planet for a very long time.

Waste-wary consumer that I am, I never throw my clothing in the trash. I really don't. Whenever something doesn't make it to the "keep-forever category" I'll either return it to the store (unworn), resell it through my blog and give the money to charity, or sell it at a local consignment shop. Anything left after that gets donated to Goodwill or another charity. So I'm ethically in the clear, right? Well, not quite. Donating to Goodwill sounds great and charitable but donating clothes, as it turns out, isn't always the good deed we think it is.

I visited the Goodwill headquarters of Central Florida in 2011 on a writing assignment for *Visit Florida*. At the time it really warmed my heart to see all these clothing donations being put to good use. Workers sorted the items, keeping the best things to sell at local Goodwill stores. Sales from the best items contribute to the local economy and provide jobs and training programs here in Central Florida. A lot of the items donated are unsellable though, and that stuff gets compacted by a machine into big bricks of clothing and "sent overseas." I always felt great knowing that when I donated clothing it was being put to good use, whether it was right here in Central Florida or across the ocean to people who "really needed it." All of this seemed completely virtuous to me, until I realized how damaging to local economies those overseas clothing donations can actually be.

Our unwanted clothing in America reaches the ends of the earth. Several tribes in Africa have words referring to clothing donations from Americans that translate loosely to "dead white man's clothing." (They assume we're dead because why else wouldn't we want the clothes?) In a tiny village in Sierra Leone, a good eight-hour drive from the closest major city (Freetown is only 119 miles away, but you can't go much faster than 10 to 15 miles an hour thanks to the condition of the roads), I saw little kids wearing Obama T-shirts and American sports team logos. If you're lucky you may even spot some "misprints," like when companies print thousands of shirts touting each team as the Super Bowl winner so they're ready to sell instantly, and then discard the losing team's T-shirts by sending them to another country.

Like we touched on in chapter 7, we are not helping anyone when we donate things that people don't actually want or need. And in the case of clothing donations, we are often doing more harm than good. When America started sending clothing donations overseas in the 1970s and 1980s, it crashed the clothing and textile industries in several African countries and in Haiti. Local artisans were pushed out by people in a different kind of business—selling our unwanted stuff.[19] Now they set up little booths on the side of the street with our clothing donations from America and disperse them to the general population. This isn't skilled work like learning to sew in a factory, which people can use for future jobs. It's also not high-paying work. And because of this industry, a part of Africa's rich heritage—the telling of family stories through beautiful fabrics—is in danger of extinction, threatened by the hand-me-down T-shirts sent over from America.

When we look closely, we find that charity stores like Goodwill and Salvation Army are overwhelmed with our donations. And third-world countries are overwhelmed with our donations. In sum, we simply have too much stuff! Our purchasing and cycling through massive amounts of clothing each year is having a destructive impact.

I have certainly looked at an item in the store and thought, *It's only fifteen dollars, so why not buy it?* It seems of little cost or risk for me to do so. But the "true cost" is that we're filling our landfills and polluting the environment, and we're drowning third-world countries with our castaways. Stephen Colbert put it best when he said (in his usual sarcastic tone):

---

19   Jacqueline Kubania, "How Second-Hand Clothing Donations Are Creating a Dilemma for Kenya," *Guardian* (Manchester), July 6, 2015, https://www.theguardian.com/world/2015/jul/06/second-hand-clothing-donations-kenya.

The global marketplace is someplace where we export work to have happen in whatever conditions we want, and then the products come back to me cheap enough to throw [away] without thinking about it.[20]

Livia Firth, the founder of Eco Age Ltd., says in the documentary *The True Cost*:

From the consumer's point of view, is it really democratic to buy a T-shirt for five dollars and a pair of jeans for twenty dollars, or are they taking us for a ride? They're making us believe we are rich and wealthy because we can buy a lot. . . . But in fact they are making us poorer, and the only person who is becoming richer is the owner of the fast-fashion brands.

If crashing economies in third-world countries and overwhelming landfills with our discarded trends are not enough motivation, then also consider this: according to Greenpeace's Detox My Fashion campaign, "the average pair of jeans requires 1,850 gallons of water to process," and "T-shirts require 715 gallons." And after going through the manufacturing process, all that water often ends up polluted.[21]

The disappearance of the Aral Sea in Kazakhstan, considered to be one of the planet's worst environmental disasters, has heavy ties to the garment industry. In the 1960s the Soviet Union developed a plan to use the body of water for irrigation, partly so that cotton, or "white gold,"

---

20 Anna Bross, "Colbert Tries Planet Money On For Size," National Public Radio website, December 11, 2013, http://www.npr.org/sections/npr-extra/2013/12/11/250176146/colbert-tries-planet-money-on-for-size.

21 Adam Matthews, "The Environmental Crisis in Your Closet," *Newsweek*, August 13, 2105, http://www.newsweek.com/2015/08/21/environmental-crisis-your-closet-362409.html.

would become a major export. They succeeded: in 1988, Uzbekistan was the world's largest exporter of cotton. But all that demand almost completely dried up the sea, and the area is now known as Aralkum Desert.

Buying more clothes not only means using up scarce resources like water and releasing tons of pollutants during the manufacturing process, the energy costs and pollution caused by shipping all these clothes across oceans plays a part as well. Think about all the energy and natural resources, gas, and oil it takes to ship denim from the manufacturer, to a warehouse, to your house. And if you've seen the documentary *Sonic Sea*, then you know that the globalization of goods and the amount of shipping, particularly in the northern hemisphere, has had another surprising effect on our environment: the increase in cargo-ship activity is making so much noise it's actually killing whales and dolphins. Ocean mammals' hearing is incredibly sensitive, and they use sonar to hunt, to know where they are going, and to communicate with one another. When cargo ships come through they create so much noise the mammals simply cannot function, and as the documentary theorizes, it drives them mad to the point of beaching themselves.

So what can we, as fashion consumers, do to help? Beyond buying less and using our clothes for as long as we can, how can we improve this dire situation?

What We Can Do

When I reflect on what feels like a world fashion crisis, it's enough to make me want to put down this book, go live in a van, and never buy another clothing item again. I'm certainly going through a bit of a fashion metamorphosis at the moment, and this chapter in particular is weighing most heavily on my heart. I very strategically put this chapter near the end of the book, though, because I needed to be able to reflect on the previous chapters to talk me off the ledge. (I'm only half kidding about living naked in the wilderness, guys!)

When I start to spiral into a tizzy about fair wages and the environment and being an ethical consumer, I have to remind myself that fashion is not inherently evil. That fabrics and colors were put here on earth as a gift by our Creator, for us to enjoy. That enjoying these things are often a very precious part of our souls, of a deeper longing to be creative. That even if I wanted to avoid clothing, I would still need to wear something (nudist colony = really not for me), and what I wear communicates so much to the world around me and the society in which I operate. Liking clothing is not necessarily vanity, and it is related to but also doesn't have to define my deepest longings to feel beautiful. That fashion is not inherently selfish, and that pampering and self-care actually helps enable us to help others. And that financially, it's entirely possible to enjoy fashion while also being fiscally responsible.

Learning about fair-trade wages and environmental impacts doesn't negate these ideas about fashion, or make them any less true. No, learning about these important issues just means that perhaps the way we embrace our love for fashion happens a little differently, especially in terms of how much we buy and what we buy. It's all about finding the right balance.

How Much We Buy

There's a huge trend in fashion right now called the capsule wardrobe. It limits the number of items you own to only a few essential items of clothing that are classics and won't go out of style. There are different ways of approaching this concept—some capsule wardrobes are replaced and updated as many times as once per season or once a month, others are more long-term. But the basic idea is to have a closet that is minimalist and utilitarian.

One real-life example of a capsule-type wardrobe is that of Steve Jobs's. As the cofounder and CEO of Apple, he was busy changing the way the world interacts with computers and inventing technology like iPods and iPhones. So he adopted a self-imposed uniform, wearing a similar black turtleneck and jeans every single day. This minimalist approach to getting dressed made sense for Steve Jobs, because like anyone, he only had so much brain power, energy, time, and money to spend; it made more sense for him to focus on revolutionizing technology during his short time on earth rather than wasting time figuring out what color tie to wear.

Choosing a uniform or a capsule wardrobe for yourself means fewer decisions to make and less time and money spent on getting dressed. It curbs worldwide problems like environmental waste. And probably my favorite capsule wardrobe benefit: it normalizes repeating outfits. It drives me crazy when magazine features make a big fuss about a celebrity wearing the same outfit twice. Because that's reality for a normal person with a normal budget! And how wasteful not to wear something more than once! I really appreciate that capsule wardrobes make it "cool" to repeat what you already own. I'm all for it and regularly embrace that practice in my own wardrobe.

In many ways I can relate to the many benefits of capsule wardrobes, because it's how I approach food. I eat the same meals and snacks every day and hardly ever go to restaurants. I see food as fuel and as a way to maintain my body in a healthy state, and that's pretty much it. I would be happy taking vitamins for sustenance and never thinking about food again. Part of me wants to embrace the capsule wardrobe and everything it stands for. It appeals to me on many levels, from my childhood of frugality to my concern for the environmental impact of the garment industry. And yet when I consider a capsule wardrobe, I picture opening the doors to my closet and finding a dry desert inside with a tumbleweed rolling by.

Perhaps you would say that life without food is no life to live at all, but I would say the same for fashion. Surely, there are days and occasions when I approach clothing in a completely utilitarian way. I've mentioned that I often wear running shorts and no makeup for errands, and beyond that I'm likely to repeat the same handful of "fun" outfits for occasions over and over. I will happily take time off from shopping or creating outfits whenever life gets busy or the season calls for it. But I also can't deny that ever-present itch to create using clothes and fashion when my schedule and budget allow for it. The whisperings of my creative soul from a young age always finds its way back to me, and I desire to fling open my closet doors and find behind them a plethora of exciting, wonderful things to answer that call.

In general, I'm attracted to colorful, embellished, and unique things, and I enjoy having many of those special items to mix together in tons of different ways. I'm not trying to blend in or save time on clothes like Steve Jobs did; I'm trying to create art, and clothing and accessories are the paints I use. For example, there are hundreds, if not thousands, of shades of the color blue. I'm not asking for all of them to be in my closet, but I easily own ten to thirty shirts in different shades of blue, and we haven't even gotten started on all the shades of pink, green, red, and yellow!

Like many visual artists, I want the entire spectrum of the rainbow in my closet, and I want to regularly add new things to my arsenal— new colors, new shapes, new styles. I'm not necessarily driven by trends (although they do fascinate me and I write about them often), but by a desire to create more art. By adding just one small item to my closet it can inspire thirty new outfits, and when a new color or a new shape becomes available at a store in my price range, I'm beyond excited to try it.

I relate so much to this poetic description of our human nature to collect beautiful and meaningful things, from a *New York Times* article by Dominique Browning called "Let's Celebrate the Art of Clutter":

I would like to submit an entirely different agenda
. . . One that acknowledges that in living, we accu-
mulate. We admire. We desire. We love. We collect.
We display.

And over the course of a lifetime, we forage, root
and rummage around in our stuff, because that is part
of what it means to be human. We treasure.

Why on earth would we get rid of our wonderful
things?

It is time to celebrate the gentle art of clutter. We
live, and we pick up things along the way: the detritus
of adventure; the vessels of mealtimes; the books and
music of a life of the mind; the pleasures of our daily
romps through the senses.

In accumulating, we honor the art of the potter,
sitting at a wheel; we appreciate the art of the writer,
sitting at a desk; we cherish the art of the painter,
standing in front of an easel.[22]

As I sit here writing, the pale pink roses my husband brought home
for me are in view. When I was younger I saw such things as frivolous
and would have admonished my husband for being wasteful, but now
I can almost tangibly feel the importance of aesthetics and its ability to
change the room. (One could say these roses give me life because their
beauty has the ability to inspire the words on my page!) Our shelf of
knickknacks and books is not far away. It's full of things we've collected
on our travels, and objects from our families that hold so much meaning and help us recall memories with great fondness.

---

22 Dominique Browning, "Let's Celebrate the Art of Clutter," *New York
Times*, May 29, 2015, https://www.nytimes.com/2015/05/31/style/lets
-celebrate-the-art-of-clutter.html.

Perhaps you've heard of Marie Kondo's method of removing clutter. Her book *The Life-Changing Magic of Tidying Up: The Japanese Art of Decluttering and Organizing* sold more than two million copies, and she now hosts decluttering conferences across the country. She recommends a method of living a more minimalistic life, called "KonMari," where you hold each item in your home in your hands and ask yourself if it "sparks joy." If it doesn't, you discard it. There are elements to her method that I appreciate. Certainly, there is a huge emphasis on stuff in our country, of buying and lugging it home with relentless repetition until our houses can no longer contain more things and we need to buy a bigger one. In general, I'm all for decluttering and owning less, I just think the items we already own are not necessarily the only or most important part of the process to focus on.

Because why not ask if something sparks joy at the point when we buy it? When I purchase decor for our home, a book for our bookshelf, or shoes for my closet, I'm making a commitment to keep that item, basically until the end of time, or at least for a very, very long time. Before you take an item home, hold it in your hand and ask, "Does this spark joy?" and "Am I willing to make a lifelong commitment to this item?" Instead of keeping only what you treasure, I'm proposing that we not buy stuff in the first place, but only acquire what we love and what we know we will treasure, now and in the future.

I like this method from April Benson, PhD, author of *To Buy or Not to Buy: Why We Overshop and How to Stop*, which recommends asking yourself these six questions each time you buy something:

1. Why am I here?
2. How do I feel?
3. Do I need this?
4. What if I wait?
5. How will I pay for it?
6. Where will I put it?

Because even as an artist who responsibly enjoys fashion on a deeper level, and as a person who likes to collect meaningful things on a bookshelf, I absolutely have a responsibility to the world around me when it comes to my purchases. I don't think we have to choose one or the other, though—I think we can be both. I don't think the answer is to dump everything and start over (there is some serious wastefulness, in fact, to doing it that way!). I think the answer lies in balance, and finding a way to enjoy our creativity and our love for colors or for collecting objects in responsible ways. When fashion is done responsibly, I think we can feel okay about having fun with it too.

I've always been meticulous about what and how much I buy. I plan out my purchases with a carefully curated budget and thoughtfulness regarding wastefulness and the longevity of an item. I've always tried to shop with respect and responsibility, but I know I've also made my share of purchasing mistakes too. I wanted to take an honest look at how I'm really doing in this area, so I did a five-year review of my clothing budget on my blog recently. I was so surprised (and disappointed) at how many of the items I no longer owned or wore! Many of them were low-quality and didn't hold up well; others I now realize were just less-than-thoughtful purchases made on a whim that I simply didn't like anymore. It was a great learning moment and an exercise I would recommend anyone try. You may be surprised at how much is circling in and out of your closet, and how quickly it goes—I know I certainly was.

Now that I'm more aware of fashion's ethical and environmental impact, I have even more motivation to do better and make better decisions. I'm now willing to spend more on one item than I ever have before. Moving forward, I plan to buy fewer pieces with my clothing budget and spend more time thoughtfully planning those purchases. I used to squeeze twenty to thirty items out of my monthly budget; now I'm aiming for five or six items per month. Which is still a lot, I know—and it doesn't include the influx of clothing that makes its way into our house because of J's Everyday Fashion through sponsorships and such. Still, it's a start—and that's the point. We absolutely must start somewhere. Even one little change in the way that we buy can add up to a huge difference.

Of course, how much we buy is only part of the equation. We also have to consider what we buy—which may have the biggest impact of all. When we consider purchasing an item, I'm proposing that we ask: What is it made of? Who made it? How were they treated? And what impact will it have on the environment?

What We Buy

When I think about revolutionizing what we buy, the two science experiments with sweaters instantly come to mind. Perhaps the easiest place to start is by buying natural fibers. Since the Federal Trade Commission requires that fiber content be listed on clothing labels, we can seek out natural fabrics fairly easily, with hopes that those materials will have a much better impact on the environment.

Think of it like a new diet. Knowing how harmful manmade fibers can be, you're backing off the synthetic materials—it's like giving up fried foods when you are trying to eat healthy. A closet full of polyester and acrylic is basically plastic, and they're not so good for the environment. Silk, wool, genuine leather, cotton, and other natural fibers are like adding some fresh veggies to your diet. They biodegrade, are arguably more comfortable, and can reduce your carbon footprint.

Admittedly, natural fibers aren't perfect—they too have their ethical and environmental downsides. Take, for example, leather. Genuine leather is more breathable when you wear it, and it biodegrades. But it requires the killing of an animal. (Vegan leather, on the other hand, doesn't involve the killing of animals but is generally made of plastics and fossil fuels.) Cotton is also debatable. It biodegrades, but 25 percent of the pesticides in the United States are used in cotton farming,[23] and these pesticides have been linked to hundreds of thousands of deaths and birth defects both here in the United States and abroad. That said, if you can find it, it's better to buy organic cotton, leathers made of fruit skins, and bamboo. And there's always trusty silk, obtained from insects like silkworms, and wool that comes from sheering sheep, both of which can be collected without harming the animal.

While determining what our clothing is made of is a breeze, the other important pieces of information—who made it and whether they were treated ethically, and how the manufacturing process impacted the environment—are not. It can be difficult to detect which companies treat workers fairly and have sound environmental practices, unless they are voluntarily touting it on their labels or through their brand messaging.

With so little information about these important topics, it's tempting to make decisions based solely on price—that is, to assume that pricier brands must be spending more on wages, working conditions, and environmental safeguards. They must be, right? With this thought in mind, I started looking at dresses in the $300 to $400 range instead of my usual $100 range. But so far the $300 dresses I've found are polyester (the same manmade fabric as many $30 dresses!), and even the "elevated" brands I've browsed don't provide any information about their wage practices on their websites. Certainly price matters to some extent (as we discussed previously, cheaply made fashion often ends up as waste), but it's not the sole determining factor. Just because you got an amazing vintage coat or a shirt on sale for $10, for example, doesn't mean it was cheaply and unethically made. The cost of an item doesn't always determine its worth.

---

23   Will Allen, "Fact Sheet on U.S. Cotton Subsidies and Cotton Production," Organic Consumers Association, February 2014, https://www.organicconsumers.org/old_articles/clothes/224subsidies.php.

Given the lack of information we consumers have, I'm taking an overall "demand evidence and think critically" approach, with plans to buy as smartly as possible. In other words, let's let companies know we are interested in how our clothing impacts the world—and let's reward good behavior with our hard-earned dollars. Fortunately, there are a couple of good resources out there that help us do this.

One such organization is FashionRevolution.org. They believe that change starts with the consumer. They organize events like Fashion Revolution Week, where people are encouraged to post photos holding a sign that says, "Who made my clothes?" as well as to make films, choreograph dances, pull stunts, hack fashion shoots, or anything that will gain the attention of the press. Throughout the year, they encourage the use of hashtags like #whomademyclothes to help get the message to retailers that we're willing to pay more for fair trade and that we have the power to withhold our purchases from brands that abuse the environment and perpetuate bad working conditions. A lot of small decisions on our part can add up to a huge impact and a large voice within the fashion industry.

Greenpeace Catwalk is another resource focused on providing environmental information. They rate brands on their commitments to eliminating chemicals and producing nontoxic fashion. As the second-largest retailer in the world, H&M often has a bad reputation for making the garment industry worse, not better, but they actually receive very high marks from Greenpeace for their environmental efforts.[24] Things like H&M's eco-conscious clothing line, and their 15-percent-off discount incentive when you hand in old clothing to one of their stores for recycling, contribute to their high score. Another creative effort getting high marks is Levi's denim made from recycled plastic bottles.

---

24 "The Detox Catwalk," Greenpeace.org, accessed June 11, 2017, http://www.greenpeace.org/international/en/campaigns/detox/fashion/detox-catwalk.

In spite of the efforts we as consumers can make, it's hard not to feel somewhat powerless when it comes to the garment industry's current impact on our world. I want stylish clothing that is biodegradable and made with fair wages—and I am very much struggling to find it. I want nothing more than a Whole Foods of ethical fashion, where I can get things in colors and styles I want, pay more for it, and feel good about it. It cannot get here soon enough.

Because let's face it: when a fair trade or environmentally friendly company just happens to make fashion and not the other way around, it's not cute. I find it very difficult to locate fair-trade companies making the styles and aesthetics that I'm shopping for. They mostly focus on basic staples, but I'm mostly looking for color, pattern, and pizzazz, so it makes shopping difficult. As a chef, if mango is an important ingredient to my dish, do I still buy it, even though I can't confirm that it's fair trade and organic? This is the question that I find myself facing every time I buy something. How do I balance these four factors?

1. What is the price?
2. Does it satisfy my fashion appetite, is it aesthetically pleasing, and is it the paint I need to complete my art?
3. Is it environmentally friendly?
4. Was it made ethically, with fair wages?

Then there's the fact that these questions can't even be considered until the most practical requirements have been met! Such as: Does it fit me? Is it comfortable? Will I be too hot or too cold wearing it? Is it practical for my lifestyle? What is the dress code where I plan to wear it? I feel as if I may never shop again if I hope to honor the entire list! I have a hard enough time finding a dress that I like that's within my budget, let alone worrying about ethical questions such as the environment and fair trade.

Certainly fashion says something about us, and I will always, to some extent, want to portray a certain aesthetic when it comes to my clothes. But I also have to consider whether my clothing is communicating something else—that I'm a sucker for fast fashion; that I don't care deeply about the human lives and the mother earth behind my clothing. I'm looking forward to putting the soul back into fashion. I'm looking forward to feeling a different connection to clothing that I've never had before, in knowing that my clothing decisions can change a life and make a great impact on the world.

I end this chapter with more questions about global responsibility than answers. I hope that the garment industry changes quickly, and that environmentally friendly practices and fair wages don't become just a passing trend but the status quo. I hope personally that I can figure out some way to balance my creative desires for getting dressed with honoring the environment and fair wages, as insurmountable as that may seem to me now. As consumers, we must believe that we can change the clothing industry and our retail options, even by implementing small changes. We can try to add one sustainable or fair-wage item to our budgets each month or each year. We can buy less and buy natural. We can "demand evidence and think critically," so that we can use that info to buy as smartly as possible. I do believe that our questions can become our answers, if we continue and persevere in our quest for solutions and the truth.

Chapter 10

Who Has the Final Say?

In the past when my career in fashion was questioned within a faith-based context, I went into full defense mode. When I was asked to "prayerfully consider modesty" or had Bible verses, like "For where your treasure is, there your heart will be also," quoted at me, I had a stocked arsenal of reasons why fashion and faith can peacefully coexist. Like arrows in a bow, I launched them one by one, until I felt that the listening party believed that I could actually, truly still love God and be a Christian while also working in the fashion industry. Pew, pew, pew, one by one, I'd launch them at the listener. Not coincidentally, these are the topics of chapters 1 through 9.

- God has a heart for beauty and the arts.
- You can serve God in your vocation, no matter the vocation.
- Fashion is a necessity, especially in an appearance-driven society.
- Style and beauty play an important role in our self-esteem and the call of our heart.
- Modesty is an incredibly complicated topic with many points of view to consider.
- Spending time on fashion is not always selfish.
- Spending money on fashion can be done faithfully and responsibly.

- Enjoying clothes can be done without being wasteful.
- We can make the world a better place with fashion, by choosing fair trade and brands with a purpose.

I shared these ideas with you in a book because I want you to be convinced as well. Not convinced of my own salvation, though. And not so that you can use these arrows to launch them at others and convince them of your salvation, either. No. I shared these ideas with you because I want you to be convinced for yourself, to help you settle your own internal battle.

Certainly fashion can creep into sinful territory, and Scripture tells us that in some ways, what others think of us does actually matter. Our good deeds, observed by men, "glorify God" (1 Peter 2:12), and "A good name is to be more desired than great wealth, favor is better than silver and gold" (Proverbs 22:1).

But before we dive into those matters of the heart, when the issue is more critical and centered on sin, let's first explore two much less serious scenarios: when a fashion choice stems from a question of personal taste or as a result of experimenting with style. Because when it's these two lighthearted topics at hand, I propose that the only defense you need against fashion feedback is a polite and genuinely sweet, "It's none of your business!"

Personal Taste: It's All Correct

Many moons ago, when I first started blogging, a woman commented on my Facebook page:

> I love that gaudy *Jersey Shore*–type style. Do you have any recommendations for stores where I can find those types of clothes?

Initially, I was floored. "Gaudy" is generally not a positive word or something you would proudly aspire to. Gaudy means too flashy and too much, akin to adding way too much salt to your food. Not to mention that at the time, Jersey Shore style was my specific barometer for figuring out when things had gone "too far." I've always loved piling on accessories, mixing prints, and experimenting with a generally loud, garish style, but I've also never wanted to be wearing anything that could be mistaken for something seen on Jersey Shore. And yet this woman was publicly and proudly aspiring to it? It completely put me in my place and was a real lightbulb moment for me.

Bringing it down to the most molecular level, I want to talk about judging personal style and taste, and who has the final say on what is right and wrong in fashion. To me, it's a pretty silly argument, and yet we have it all the time (or at least in my world we do, because it's one of the side effects that comes with a prescription for blogging). But is there even such a thing as right and wrong in an art like fashion in the first place?

Let's consider an example from another art: singing. When I'm getting ready in the morning sometimes I unabashedly belt out praise and worship. I don't have any misgivings about my talent. I know my voice isn't great, and yet I don't hold anything back; I'm pretty sure the neighbors can hear me. One could certainly argue that I'm belting out the "wrong" notes repeatedly, but does that really mean I should stop? Or is that missing the point completely? Because that's how I feel about style. So what if my outfit isn't hitting all the right notes all the time? I often poke fun at what I'm wearing, but I am also completely confident in my style because of the joy that it brings me. (I call it "the audacity to enjoy myself.") I don't believe that things like fashion and singing are only for an elite bunch who always get it "right" every time, and when we consider it from this angle, perhaps right and wrong in fashion is actually quite arbitrary?

That old Facebook comment helped me begin to understand that we should feel free embrace our "gaudy," whatever that means to us. I believe we all have different style tastes that are innate, just like with food preferences. You are born liking a simple, uncomplicated style of clothing, or you are born liking a messy, flashy style of clothing, or something in between. Simple or complicated, neutral or colorful: it's all a part of your fashion soul. It's a sliding scale, and wherever you land is totally fine; the entire spectrum is open for you to explore.

Gaudy ←——→ Plain

I would describe myself as pretty far into the "gaudy" side of the spectrum. As a fashion blogger, I often receive comments on my outfits telling me that I need to tone it down or remove an accessory. Not because the commenter thinks I'm being sinful, but as a matter of good taste. I understand where this comes from—after all, I was the one totally hating on Jersey Shore for a minute! I can understand when someone goes too far and you want to correct them by suggesting they wear a little less makeup or tone down the sequins, or by pointing out that's way too many colors for one outfit. There's something about being on Team Plain that can drive you a little crazy when you see Team Gaudy. I totally get having those thoughts.

Where this idea of universally accepting others' fashion sense starts to get confusing is when we want to speak our personal taste to the world. And as much as I believe we should embrace our own personal taste by wearing what speaks to us, I also believe we should feel free to share our point of view with others! However, in doing so, we sometimes consciously and unconsciously attack the other side and don't allow anything but our own personal taste to be valid. You should feel confident that you like gaudy or don't like gaudy and can share that opinion, but *how* you share your very valid opinion is everything.

When I first started shooting TV segments on syndicated morning show Daytime a few years ago, I had to work through this complicated landscape wrought with land mines. How should I approach sharing my fashion opinion on national television, as part of a *Fashion Police*–type segment that critiques celebrity outfits? A good place to start, I thought, is to only say things that I would be happy to hear about my own outfits. I tend to joke around a lot and say some outlandish things, like the time I compared a celebrity's dress to a bed skirt during a TV segment. But that's also the tone and type of observation I make on my blog about my own clothes—I've joked that my outfits look like Snow White, the Hamburglar, or a prisoner (it was a close call that time), and I once used a Hostess cupcake as my "inspiration photo" (that's what I call the photos—usually of celebrities or from catalogs—that inspire the outfits I put on my blog). There's no harm in dressing like a delicious cupcake or a bed linen in my book. If we can't sometimes wear a bed-skirt dress, then what are we doing with our lives?! (Taking them too seriously, I assume.)

The most crucial distinction for me, though, is whether sharing my own opinion is squashing the other side of the spectrum. Are we leaving space for other opinions to be valid? It's the difference between saying, "I don't like cilantro in my dish, so I'll make a substitute," and "You are so disgusting for liking cilantro! It's just plain wrong. No one should ever eat cilantro, ever!" Because ultimately, our ability to choose between black and white or light and dark means that each must exist. If we feel we must insist that one side is wrong, we actually eliminate the ability for our own side to be right. For example, if we say "too much salt" and want to rid the world of salt, our personal choice of not using salt is no longer a choice. If everyone is forced to do it, then our own point of view is no longer ours—rather, it's the norm.

And yet so often style feedback insists that our way is the only way. Consider for a moment the difference between "this is my point of view, different from yours, and I'm sharing it with you" and "your point of view is wrong, only my point of view can be right." I may not like the outfit a celebrity is wearing, and I may never choose to wear a bed-skirt dress myself, but I also share that sentiment with the utmost respect in another's right to wear that dress, leaving space for their opinion. I try to never say a style choice is wrong, I only say that it's not right for me. And no matter my opinion, I would encourage them to wear it if that's what feels the best to them and brings them joy. Giving space to the person wearing it, and allowing them to have their own different opinion from yours, makes all the difference in the world.

Not only are those differing style tastes a precious part of our souls to be celebrated, but all too often, stifling fashion taste perpetuates the idea that women shouldn't take up too much space in society. Women are told to not be loud, to not be assertive, and to be skinny (quite literally, "Don't take up space!"). Women managers are "bossy," and women who dress too flashy need to "tone it down." When we say these things, are we really just buying into the part of our culture that tells us to keep women quiet? Please let the loud dressers do their thing and take up all the space they want. I hope to be a shining example of that on my blog—I certainly like to pile it on most days!

Author Glennon Doyle Melton puts it so well in this quote, originally posted on her blog Momastery, but now a popular meme: "It's not a woman's job to get smaller and smaller until she disappears so the world can be more comfortable."

I've mentioned previously that basic items like jeans, a trench coat, or a pair of simple black pumps are great foundations for any woman's wardrobe, but they also kind of bore me to tears. In my closet, "sizzle" is the reigning champion—the fun things that really get my heart pumping, like a beautiful cobalt blouse, a fun polka-dot skirt, or bright yellow heels. I might be at the mall shopping for something basic when a neon skirt from across the store starts calling my name. *Gotta have that!* If I were to challenge myself to a capsule collection containing only ten items, I'd likely go for ten super-fun party dresses like an irresponsible toddler. And I would just wear those flashy dresses every day, no matter where I was going, because that's what I'm drawn to. Tying it back to chapter 2, these tastes and style preferences are something I believe are innate—I was born with them in my heart—and those desires should be celebrated and not squashed.

To that reader who shared her love for Jersey Shore style (or cilantro or using a lot of salt, if you're sticking with the food analogies), I wanted to say, "You go, girl! You love gaudy? You should fully embrace that! Let all that garishness shine, and don't worry about what Team Plain thinks, even when it hurts their eyes a little. Please feel free to take up as much space as you want with your fashion."

And to anyone who prefers a much simpler way of dressing, I also say, "You go, girl! You love plain? You should fully embrace that! Live your life happily in basics and don't feel an ounce of guilt for not dressing as loudly as other people do." I'm so thankful that that reader inspired me to embrace everyone's preferences, no matter where they land.

Author and spiritual leader Danielle LaPorte says:

> You will always be too much of something for someone: too big, too loud, too soft, too edgy. If you round out your edges, you lose your edge. Apologize for mistakes. Apologize for unintentionally hurting someone—profusely. But don't apologize for being who you are.[1]

We should never, ever feel guilty for liking or not liking cilantro, for being flashy or being a plain dresser. But in the same way that we take ownership over our fashion tastes and opinions, we should respect the

---

1   "The Positivity of Pride," *Danielle LaPorte* (blog), accessed June 11, 2017, http://www.daniellelaporte.com/the-positivity-of-pride.

fashion opinions of others. Fashion is meant to be fun, and engaging in a discourse over differing fashion opinions should not be threatening. I love hearing why someone doesn't like something about my outfit, because they are entitled to their artistic opinions too. And that difference of opinions is truly the spice of life.

Fashion Mistakes Are Awesome

I'm a perfectionist, so when I make mistakes it tends to grate on my every last nerve. Just imagine how carefree and wonderful life would be if we could go through each day never making any mistakes? But who am I kidding—that's a far-off fantasy. Because I make mistakes all the time. I lose my temper, I forget things, I'm messy, and possibly my most frequent offense—I make fashion mistakes!

Thankfully, I once heard a story about a friend of a friend that became my modus operandi for dealing with mistakes. This friend was a therapist, and he suffered from pretty significant bouts of perfectionism. To counteract those thoughts, he had a really interesting method. After he had cleaned up the room at AA meetings, for example, he would stick his thumb in peanut butter, smear it on the table, and leave. *Take that, perfectionism!*

When it comes to most things in life—fashion, art, cooking, or writing a blog post—I've adopted a similar approach: you absolutely can't be afraid to make mistakes or fail. When I started my blog, I decided to go with the smearing-peanut-butter technique and put all my fashion mistakes out there for everyone to see. One time I posted a collage of what I considered to be my worst fashion fails and super-imposed it with a graphic declaring in the text, "Fail, please try again." I enjoy poking fun at my mistakes, especially when the subject is as lighthearted as fashion!

Call me the Julia Child of the fashion-blogging world, but I don't come from a fashion background and along the way, I knew I would drop plenty of turkeys on the floor. (Julia Child was known for dropping food on the floor and joyfully brushing it off as she was cooking on TV. It's actually a bit of an urban legend because she never dropped a turkey, but the general spirit of her PBS cooking show was along these lines.) This makes some people uncomfortable—they would rather see fashion media that presents a more perfect image. But it's always been my hope that some women would find the imperfect part of me, and of *J's Everyday Fashion*, inspirational, and would dive in and drop some of their own turkeys along the way with me. Not to mention that if I waited until I looked perfect in pictures or had the best outfit or the most compelling text, then I would have probably never published a single blog post. I just don't think picture-perfect fashion 100 percent of the time was my calling in life, guys—I mean, look at some of the outfits I post!

Coming from a place of not taking fashion too seriously and not worrying about fashion mistakes will certainly help keep things light and airy for you. It will also, I've discovered, help you become a better dresser. Because the first rule of Cool Club is that you don't care about Cool Club, and fashion is the same. By not caring, you actually get better.

When I was a personal shopper for a short time, I felt like my role was basically to be a "cheerleader for mistakes." All I really did was talk people into trying things on that they thought would look horrible. Our sessions would start with me asking them what they absolutely wouldn't wear—like the color yellow or statement necklaces, for example—and would end with me insisting that they try those things on. They almost always loved those things the most and bought what they thought they hated on the spot! I know it's uncomfortable to take a fashion risk or try something new, but it's honestly the best thing you can do style-wise.

Fashion mistakes are necessary to learn and grow, and ultimately they are how you become a better dresser.

We're so afraid of making mistakes or wasting time on a possible failed idea that we often won't even try, though. But those seemingly "risky" style statements are often the ones we wind up loving the most. Sometimes I post pictures of out-of-the-box fashion items I'm considering buying. (My struggle isn't with feeling brave about wearing them, I'm just trying to figure out if I can get enough use out of them to justify their cost!) I keep playing the game of fashion roulette, because it's where the biggest reward lies. Those "unsure" style risks pay off and sometimes become the best thing I've ever bought. Surely, I could just buy something safe, but with the greatest (fashion) risk, lies the greatest (fashion) reward.

If you're still not convinced that fashion mistakes are for you, then consider this: at the end of the day, no matter how amazing your outfit is, or how safe it is, someone won't like it. Going back to our food analogy, some people just don't like cilantro, no matter what you do. (Not unlike real-life cilantro, which has been scientifically proven to taste like soap to some people.) So if you adopt a uniform and only wear basic items, someone will find that style boring and not really their thing. If you jazz it up and go nuts, someone won't like that, either. But this idea that artistic points of view can be so drastically different—where one sees beauty, another sees a mistake—gives us all the permission we need to make fashion decisions freely. Since we are never going to be able please everyone, then why try for that goal at all?

There are a few notable exceptions (like the ones discussed in chapter 3's exploration of how we communicate using our clothes and chapter 6's discussion on modesty), but otherwise, if you want to wear it, then wear it! A friend said to me the other day, "I'm too old to wear that," and I replied, "Says who?!" If you decide you don't want to wear it, then that's your decision, but the only person who can tell you you're too old to wear something is you. Confidence is everything, and if you love what you are wearing, then that's more than half the battle.

Certainly, it's possible to get into hot water with fashion. Vanity, greed, frivolousness, and immodesty are serious issues of the heart that should be considered. And while I certainly recommend a polite, "It's none of your business!" on the topic of personal taste and fashion mistakes, the response becomes a lot more complicated, and is not always a sufficient coverall, when the question of sin is raised.

Judging Each Other's Fashion Sins

Have you ever seen *Holy Rollers: The True Story of Card Counting Christians?* It's a documentary about a group of Christians who run a blackjack ring as their primary source of income. Working as a team, they secure outside investors who provide capital, and players share profits to maximize chances of high returns. Many of the people involved are also pastors, and all of them are active in their Christian faith—attending church, reading the Bible, and praying together.

The blackjack players in the documentary are adamant that they are not sinning, even though one could argue that the Bible forbids gambling. Being the self-deprecating jokester that I am, I couldn't help but make parallels between their story and a book about why it's okay for Christians to go shopping and enjoy fashion (a.k.a. the book you are reading right now)—perhaps both sound equally far-fetched to you. In the film, they talk about how God guides every hand of blackjack they play, and they are completely convinced that two-day benders in a casino away from their families is not gambling. Still, this didn't sit completely right with me. In the same way, I know that my shopping habits and my "justifications" for enjoying fashion in this book will absolutely not sit right with everyone. Which is exactly where this chapter comes in. Because who has the final say on what is right and wrong—that is, in terms of sin—when it comes to our fashion choices?

For example, there's this photo of me in my closet. I'm sitting on a zebra-print stool, with a rainbow of shoes scattered across the floor. I'm holding a pair of high heels in the air, with a look of pure joy on my face. I appear to be basking in the glory of mass consumerism. I look like I might have a shopping addiction, and that I'm probably pretty narcissistic. But what if you knew that every pair of shoes in the picture cost under fifty dollars? And that I spend three to six times my clothing budget every month on charity? And that my career is all about empowering women and making a positive difference in the fashion industry? Would that change how you view that picture?

Because we simply can't know. Even when you learn additional facts about someone, or look at their checking account, you can't know another person's heart completely. Let's consider another example. Let's say that a woman named Harriett spent $1 million on clothes last year, and she is holding a $10,000 purse in an Instagram photo. I'll admit that I struggle with this. Some people might struggle with coveting her purse, but I struggle with judging Harriett for owning that purse. (It's interesting to note here how both actions are a sin, though, right? You can commit both, by coveting her bag and judging her for it at the same time.)

But what if Harriett spent $1 million on clothes, and donated $100 million to charity in the same year? Does that change things?

In these moments, I try to remind myself how much my own spending has changed dramatically over the years. My limit for a purse, for example, used to be about $100. But now my cap is around $250, an amount that would've felt completely outlandish a short time ago. My income and lifestyle are different now, and who am I to say that they won't change again and again? And that after many little baby steps of spending more and more on purses, I won't actually own a $10,000 purse one day, the same one I judged Harriett for?

There are some schools of thought that say if we are not "standing up to sin" and correcting our fellow humans around us, we have become soft, and our faith is wishy-washy. The doctrine and the faith that I subscribe to, though, is the one we see in John 8: "Let any one of you who is without sin be the first to throw a stone at her" (NIV). That's right out of Jesus's mouth, so who am I to judge blackjack-playing Christians or someone with millions of dollars in clothes? I am not without sin myself, and even if I have literally never stepped foot in a casino, or have a tiny clothing budget, it's simply not for me to judge. We've all read John 8, and yet how often are we Pharisees in life—calling out each other's sins, fashion and otherwise? Dragging someone to the feet of Jesus, demanding that they be stoned, or picking up stones and pelting the person without a second thought?

> The teachers of the law and the Pharisees brought in a woman caught in adultery. They made her stand before the group and said to Jesus, "Teacher, this woman was caught in the act of adultery. In the Law Moses commanded us to stone such women. Now what do you say?" They were using this question as a trap, in order to have a basis for accusing him.
>
> But Jesus bent down and started to write on the ground with his finger. When they kept on questioning him, he straightened up and said to them, "Let any one of you who is without sin be the first to throw a stone at her." Again he stooped down and wrote on the ground.
>
> At this, those who heard began to go away one at a time, the older ones first, until only Jesus was left, with the woman still standing there. Jesus straightened up and asked her, "Woman, where are they? Has no one condemned you?"

"No one, sir," she said.

"Then neither do I condemn you," Jesus declared.

"Go now and leave your life of sin." (John 8:3–11, NIV)

Matthew 7:1–2 also cautions us against judging others, saying: "Do not judge, or you too will be judged. For the same way that you judge others, you will be judged, and with the measure you use, it will be measured to you" (NIV).

Putting ourselves in Harriett's shoes, or in the position of the adulterous woman in John 8 for a moment, we also shouldn't participate in the judging when it happens to us. I mentioned that in the past when my career in fashion had been questioned within a faith-based context, I went into full defense mode. Sometimes "in case of emergency," I am tempted to "break glass" and pull out arrows to defend myself, but I laid down the bow when I realized one day that I don't need to convince anyone around me anymore.

It would be dangerous for me to write a book seeking approval for my own fashion actions. While, admittedly, I don't think I have it *all* figured out—I will always be interested in self-monitoring and doing better—I'm also happily stepping out of the competition of who can do faith or "fashion and faith" the best. Call it irony, call it hypocrisy, or call it whatever you'd like, but the girl writing the book on fashion and faith may not be the one living fashion and faith to the absolute best or the most extreme, and I'm completely okay with that.

One of the more practical reasons for not judging or engaging in each other's fashion sins is so that we avoid legalism, or merit-based faith, which makes "doing good" a competition. As a naturally competitive person, I have always wanted to be the best at everything. In certain seasons of life, like when I was a teenager, I committed myself to living a sparse fashion existence and attended church six times a week (more than anyone else, assuredly—eye roll), not realizing that getting caught up in that kind of competition does not serve God or anyone else and only swells one's own ego. Instead of receiving grace as a gift available to all of us equally, I wanted to win the gold star for most devout Christian. I was completely missing the point, laid out in Ephesians 2:8: "For by grace you have been saved through faith. And this is not your own doing; it is the gift of God" (ESV).

These days, I've settled the issue of fashion and faith in my heart and feel that I'm not sinning, and that's enough for me. Yes, sometimes my actions might look sinful to someone else—I shop and buy things, I care about clothing, and I enjoy putting together outfits. But the nature of being a human means that we are sinning constantly, sometimes without even realizing it. It says in Romans 3:23, "For all have sinned and fall short of the glory of God" (ESV), and in Ecclesiastes 7:20, "Surely there is not a righteous man on earth who does good and never sins" (ESV).

To me, being a Christian does not mean you are perfect. As I see it, upholding a life of faith means that we are willing to identify and admit our sins, that we seek grace and forgiveness, that we take action to do better in the future, and that the fruit of the Spirit is evident in our lives—joy, love, patience, kindness, and gentleness. (Still working on that patience fruit during rush hour, for sure.)

So how much, then, should we care about what others think? As I look to Scripture, I do recognize that the Bible seems, at times, to contradict itself on this topic. John 8 makes it clear that judging one another's sin is not recommended, and that we should not seek the approval of men: "Am I now trying to win the approval of human beings, or of God? Or am I trying to please people? If I were still trying to please people, I would not be a servant of Christ" (Galatians 1:10, NIV).

But the Bible also says that "A good name is more desirable than great riches; to be esteemed is better than silver or gold" (Proverbs 22:1, NIV), and Paul was vigilant that he not be discredited in his handling of money for the poor in 2 Corinthians 8:20–21: "[We are] taking precaution so that no one will discredit us in our administration of this generous gift; for we have regard for what is honorable, not only in the sight of the Lord, but also in the sight of men" (NASB).

In 1 Peter 2:12, Peter tells us we should care what outsiders think because it glorifies God: "Live such good lives among the pagans that, though they accuse you of doing wrong, they may see your good deeds and glorify God on the day he visits us." (NIV)

So what gives? While it can seem at times that the Bible has totally mixed messages on this topic, it also makes perfect sense that what others think of us both matters and doesn't matter at the same time. As Christians, we may sin (even without knowing it), but we should also strive to be a light to others. In other words, it's not my job to judge your fashion or to allow you to judge mine, but I will strive to live a good life and be a good example in the area of fashion and faith anyway, because the Bible calls me to do so.

In the documentary I mentioned at the beginning of this section, one of the blackjack players is arrested, and the police officer asks the group what's to keep them from robbing their employer blind, because they could easily walk away with the tens of thousands of dollars and just say they lost it playing blackjack. The player responds, "Because we're Christians." Surely, the type of blackjack ring that they developed isn't common, because it would be very easy to steal in that situation. But in this case the system worked, because as Christians the players were dedicated to following the commandments to not steal and to be honest. To the outside world their blackjack playing may have looked, at first glance, the same as anyone else's, but they were upholding the characteristics of the Christian faith and are ultimately being a light to those around them. (In an unlikely place for sure—a casino—but a light, nonetheless.)

In a 2001 article titled "Does It Matter What Others Think?" John Piper points out that any feedback we may receive about being sinful is not necessarily "a sign of our unfaithfulness or a lack of love," because Jesus often received the same type of feedback.[2] He says:

> The litmus test of Christ in our lives . . . is not the opinion of others. We want them to see Christ in us and love him . . . But we know they may be blind to Christ and resistant to Christ. So they may think of us just what they thought of him . . . Jesus wanted men to admire him and trust him. But he did not change who he was in order to win their approval. Nor can we.
>
> Yes, we want people to see us with approval when we are displaying that Jesus is infinitely valuable to us, but we dare not make the opinion of others the measure of our faithfulness. They may be blind and resistant to truth. Then the reproach we bear is no sign of our unfaithfulness or lack of love.

Which is where this book comes in. It may not be a justification to you for my actions. It may not be a justification that you can use in your defense to others. But it is a guide for those who want their fashion to look different to the outside world, and for those who want to honor their faith. I do want the clothes I wear to be representative of the values that I hold. While I can't and shouldn't engage in the opinions of others, I can and will strive to live a life full of enough "fruit of the Spirit" to make one seriously impressive fruit salad.

John Piper summarizes this tricky balance, and why it deeply matters:

---

2   John Piper, "Does It Matter What Others Think?," DesiringGod (website), posted June 20, 2001, accessed June 11, 2017, http://www.desiringgod .org/articles/does-it-matter-what-others-think.

Our aim in life is for "Christ to be magnified in our bodies whether by life or by death" (Philippians 1:19–20). In other words . . . we do care—really care—about what others think of Christ. Their salvation hangs on what they think of Christ. And our lives are to display his truth and beauty. So we must care what others think of us as representative of Christ. Love demands it.

Our real-life mistakes and our fashion mistakes alike could all do well with a little love and kindness in the world today. In a 2016 post on his website PastorRick.com, Pastor Rick Warren says, "Love is not saying I approve of everything you do. Love is saying I accept you in spite of what you do." In Romans 15:7, it says, "Accept one another, then, just as Christ accepted you, in order to bring praise to God" (NIV). At some point we have to block out the noise. We are free from a merit-based religion, or having to perform to earn salvation, and we are free from justifying our decisions to anyone but God. (A polite "It's none of your business" to others could also work here, or just not engaging in accusations about sin at all.) So how do we justify those decisions to Him? How do we determine whether something enters into sinful territory? And how should we monitor our thoughts and actions when it comes to fashion and faith?

When Fashion Is Wrong: Our Spiritual Guide

At what point does fashion become a sin? I've been reflecting on this question for what feels like a very long time, and I don't think the answer comes from people around us. It's messy, and it's complicated. (For example, do people know they are sinning and just don't care? Or are they unaware that they are sinning?) The only conclusion I can come to is that it's not my conclusion to draw. There's only one opinion on the subject of fashion and faith that matters, and that is God's. The guidance, gentle nudges, and corrective instructions He gives me are my call to obey on these topics.

Maybe you feel responsibility to correct others' form or believe that I should too, but I believe that Jesus asks us to leave that determination completely up to Him. I can't recommend a certain way for you to approach fashion and faith in your life, because it's just not for me to say. I hope to pose a lot of questions for you. I hope to provide some starting points and Scriptures that speak to the many topics and issues that arise around the question of fashion and faith for you—but beyond that, it's a conversation that you should have with God.

The best advice I can confidently give you is to seek God's wisdom in your life. Ask for that gentle nudge from Him that guides us to the right place. Praying the prayer of Psalm 139:23–24 will lead us to answers in our hearts when it comes to our own fashion journey: "Search me, God, and know my heart; test me and know my anxious thoughts. See if there is any offensive way in me, and lead me in the way everlasting" (NIV).

It's not necessarily a one-time check-in but a fluid, ongoing conversation with God about the condition of our hearts. I've mentioned the way in which my own fashion journey is taking a new turn. It's evolving greatly from being all about the cheapest clothes all the time, which I used to believe was being a good steward of money and the best way I could honor God with my creative passion for clothes. Gentle nudges from God have opened my eyes and led me to caring more and more about where and how my clothing was made, and whether the process is environmentally friendly. And I have every reason to believe that my mind will change on the subject of fashion and faith and will take a new form in the future, as I gather more information and think critically. Any opinions in this book are likely to change, and should—we must always be flexible and willing to change our actions and our thoughts, as we seek God's command and as the world and the fashion industry change at a rapid pace.

If you have sought God's wisdom and Scriptures, heeded that advice, and are still feeling guilty about fashion, then you may be experiencing the guilt monster and whispers from the Enemy. Guilt is not a good thing, and it does not come from God—He never wants us to live a lifeless or dispassionate existence. Everything about the Bible, everything about Jesus dying on the cross, is about freedom and grace and not about condemnation and guilt.

In Psalm 103:8–12, it says:

> The Lord is merciful and gracious, slow to anger and abounding in steadfast love. He will not always chide, nor will he keep his anger forever. He does not deal with us according to our sins, nor repay us according to our iniquities. For as high as the heavens are above the earth, so great is his steadfast love toward those who fear him; as far as the east is from the west, so far does he remove our transgressions from us. (ESV)

And in 1 John 1:9: "If we confess our sins, he is faithful and just to forgive us our sins and to cleanse us from all unrighteousness" (ESV).

This may come as great news if you, like me, have spent days, months, and even years holding your head in shame about certain events in your life. As a young believer, I really knew how to dish out judgment, especially in the area of divorce, so when I went through one myself, it almost destroyed me. Or, rather, I almost destroyed myself by heaping so much guilt and shame on myself.

Even the most amicable divorce is still the most painful experience you can imagine. It can be painful for different reasons, but for me a lot of that pain came directly from guilting and shaming myself in a faith-based context. The first time I went to therapy, I talked for forty-five minutes straight before my therapist finally interrupted, "Do you realize you've been telling me it's all your fault for the last forty-five minutes?" I blamed myself for everything and took on 100 percent of the burden, even though that's not a logical conclusion to draw. I truly thought I was being a "good Christian" by punishing myself repeatedly.

The thing that finally snapped me out of the vicious cycle of self-shaming was a question my friend Kyle posed. He said, "You know it's a real slap in the face to not accept Jesus's forgiveness for your mistakes, right? He died on a cross for you, and you aren't willing to accept that because you got a divorce?" And you know what? He was right. And when I released that judgment from my own life, I also released the judgment I had placed on others around me for being divorced. It was the best silver lining from a bad situation I could've asked for.

After that experience, I now see God's instructions about divorce, or any of His commandments, in a much different light. I believe He instructs us in a way that you would tell a child not to touch a hot stove—because He knows how much it will hurt us. I believe He comes from a place of love and not harsh judgment. The same way a parent would urge us not focus on materialism or vanity, He wants us to keep our purchases in check, and to build a foundation on our inner beauty, because doing so is ultimately what's best and most healthy for our well-being.

I hope what you take away from this book is a trove of arrows, not for you to use toward others but for your own internal battle against the Enemy when he whispers in your ear that you can't be fashionable and love God at the same time. I hope to convince you that beauty is an important part of your soul and one you should feel free to explore, with plenty of Scriptures to back that up. I hope that you can find confidence in these topics so that when the stones from others come, you feel strong and confident in your faith, salvation, and the approval that stems from Jesus Christ. And that you'll use that genuinely polite defense when you need it: "It's none of your business!"

When it comes to bucking the system and going against the status quo, in some ways I'm the ultimate rebel. I did everything as opposite from the fashion industry as I possibly could on my blogging journey. But standing up for myself within my Christian faith has been much harder. In writing this book, I feel I have finally found my voice. Admonish me for enjoying an art that I know in my bones that I was made to enjoy, but I have examined the evidence. I have prayerfully considered what the Bible has to say. And while different denominations may tell me I'm wrong, if I listen to the one voice I know is the Truth, and study Jesus and His teachings, then I know I will come out just fine. Nothing makes me feel more connected to Jesus than this art in my soul, and I finally feel confident enough to declare what a blessed thing fashion is in my life. Studying the tough questions raised in this book has made my faith considerably stronger. Clothing, it seems, has brought me much closer to God, not farther away from Him.

And so I hope that you too will go forward and let your fashion flag fly. (Yes, even at church.) I pledge to always be a champion for you on your journey. My prayer for you on the road of fashion and faith is to embrace your longing, desires, passions, and talent that were put there for a reason; to seek God's wisdom in all things, and in all things find moderation; and most of all, to find, once and for all, a reconciliation between fashion (and all things creative) and your faith, personal values, and global responsibility.

It's a lifelong journey. And I'm rooting for you!

About the Author

Jeanette Johnson writes about style full-time on her popular blog, *J's Everyday Fashion*, offering practical tips and tricks for real women—with real budgets—as they navigate their daily personal style journeys. In addition to blogging, she regularly appears on morning shows, and does a host of public appearances and speaking engagements. She and her husband live in Orlando. For more on Jeanette and her work, visit www.jseverydayfashion.com.